mum's THE WORD

THE HIGH-FLYING ADVENTURES OF EVE BRANSON

By Eve Branson
with Holly Peppe

AuthorHouse™ UK Ltd.
500 Avebury Boulevard
Central Milton Keynes, MK9 2BE
www.authorhouse.co.uk
Phone: 08001974150

Published by AuthorHouse 2/19/2013

ISBN: 978-1-4772-4581-1 (sc)
ISBN: 978-1-4772-4582-8 (hc)
ISBN: 978-1-4772-4583-5 (e)

authorHOUSE®

This book is dedicated to my dear late husband
Ted and to our children—Richard, Vanessa and
Lindy— who enriched our lives beyond words.

And to all the other ever-hopeful writers
around the world—never give up!

FOREWORD

I think most sons think their mothers are extraordinary. But in the case of mine, well, she is!

I wrote a letter to a number of friends and family inviting them to come and stay for two weeks on our island Necker last summer. Everyone responded positively except Mum. "I may be able to move my diary around and make three or four days," she said. "I'll get back to you!"

Not bad for an 88-year-old but as you'll realise once you've read this book, she has always lead a "full on" life and the rest of us have just had to do our best to keep up with her. How on earth she found time in her schedule to write *Mum's The Word*, I'll never know!

Mum is the Mum who is known for dropping her six-year-old son off at the side of the road and telling him to make his own way to Granny's house. Today she would have been arrested. Then, she was determined to see her children standing on their own two feet.

I wouldn't swap her for any other Mum and our whole family has been so fortunate to have had such an inspirational woman guiding us all. *Mum's The Word* will give you a glimpse in to how she ticks. I'm sure you'll enjoy it.

Mum surrounds herself with young people and some of her best friends are half her age and trying to keep up with her. One of her very best friends, Holly Peppe, has held her hand through the process of writing this book and deserves lots of hugs from us all.

Richard Branson
Necker Island
January 2013

PREFACE

When I first visited Eve Branson at Cakeham Manor many years ago, she mentioned that she had kept a daily journal that was hidden away somewhere in the carefully restored 13th century house. She led me down a flight of red-carpeted steps, across a hand-hewn York stone floor and through a massive oak door that opened into a formal dining room. Life-sized portraits of a handsome junior barrister, decked out in legal robes and wig—her husband Ted—and a stunning young actress in a strapless flowered gown—Eve herself—stared at one another across a long wooden table surrounded by faded pink velvet Queen Anne chairs.

Eve switched on the light and a row of brown cardboard boxes came into view, lining the sideboard and walls and stacked in all corners of the room. I felt like an explorer discovering buried treasure! Opening box after box, I found bundles of neatly typed manuscripts from a lifetime of writing: novels, screenplays, essays, travel articles, children's stories and finally, her personal journal—a daily diary of more than 900 pages.

Among the revelations in that journal, which is the basis for this book, are details of her early life as a wife and mother and evidence of a lifelong entrepreneurial drive, clearly inherited by her children, that first moved her—at age 10—to set up shop selling rabbits and teaching ballet. Reading through booklet after booklet of journal entries, labelled by year and bound by white string, I knew the challenge was on: here was a writer whose spirited voice and inspiring story needed to be shared.

Writing is a lonely business, but the many enjoyable hours Eve and I have spent together, shaping the story of her singular life, have made it less so. Eve is a natural writer with a positive outlook that is perfectly balanced by her own poetic acceptance of daily reality: "Life can't be all travel and roses."

Holly Peppe
New York City
January 2013

INTRODUCTION

How I love writing! It has been one of the most rewarding and humbling tasks I've ever set for myself. In spite of having limited scholastic education, I was always writing something. Early each morning I would scratch and scrawl and revise entries in my diary and continue whenever I could find a few quiet moments of my own—sitting on a plane, in a beach hut, at the hairdresser's or at a table in my garden.

Yet I was always hesitant to send out my work for publication, frightened that a rejection would discourage me from continuing to write. I did have some success, as several of my travel articles about visits to Spain, Italy, Menorca, Morocco and other places appeared in the *Daily Telegraph* and *Daily Mail on Sunday*. And here at last is my memoir, a story packed with clues about the origins of the adventurous spirit that runs through our family.

My late husband Ted and I shared a glorious life for the rather daunting total of 62 years. After raising our own three children—Richard, Lindy and Vanessa—we enjoyed watching our 11 grandchildren pursue their various interests including entrepreneurship, music, medicine, helicopter search and rescue, photography and film production. We delighted in seeing Richard's Virgin businesses expand and following the progress of Lindy, a highly accomplished painter, sculptor, and potter, and Vanessa, a contemporary art collector, curator, artist representative, and hotelier.

Thanks to Richard, who always invited the family to join the fun on Virgin's inaugural flights and to witness his various record-setting attempts, we enjoyed travel adventures throughout the world. But why not explore another galaxy too? In 2008, he called to ask my permission to use "Eve" as the name of the mother ship in his Virgin Galactic company that will launch people to the edge of space, where weightlessness begins. I accepted this undeserved but much appreciated honor—after all, one can't possibly send a mother ship skyward without a mother inside! I was also happy to accept Richard's challenge to make history together. One of my grandsons, using a photo from my youth, designed a rather voluptuous image of me that appears on the side of the aircraft. Heading toward the heavens to release the first rocket full of "Virgin astronauts" should give me much more to write about.

When friends learn I've written my memoir, they sometimes say, "I wouldn't want other people to read about my life." But I have a different view. I think writing about your own life provides an opportunity to reflect on lessons learned and gives your family new insights into how your history helped to shape their future.

Finally, a disclaimer is in order before you turn another page: what you'll find here is my version of events according to my memories and journals—my apologies to those who may have different recollections!

Eve Branson
Cakeham Manor
Chichester, England
January 2013

MUM'S
THE
WORD

CHAPTER 1

ONE GENERALLY BEGINS ONE'S MEMOIRS with earliest recollections, mixed perhaps with stories related by family and friends. I decided to depart from this tradition and begin my story with that of my mother, the late Dorothy Constance, née Jenkins, a grand lady born in Edinburgh in 1898. She experienced two world wars, fearlessly faced many challenges and lived a full and energetic life that ended just shy of a century. At the age of 90, Mother had appeared twice in the Guinness Book of World Records.

My adventurous nature, which has shaped not only my life but also the lives of my children—Richard, Lindy and Vanessa—can easily be traced to my mother, who loved adventure, dancing and sports. In her teens, she had dived off the roof of the Drumsheugh Baths in Edinburgh! As a young woman, she had been team captain in hockey, tennis and golf and was awarded a bronze medal in skating. She stayed active throughout her life—indeed, when she was in her 60s and 70s, she received 18 medals and awards including two supreme awards in ballroom and Latin dancing. At 89, she became the oldest person in Britain to pass the advanced Latin American ballroom dancing examination.

Age did not deter her love for competition: at 96, she drove a hole-in-one at Barton on Sea Golf Club. That day, having heard the news, Richard took a helicopter to the club and treated the members to champagne, somewhat upsetting the grand old lady when all the attention shifted over to her grandson!

That same year, she met the Queen at Buckingham Palace. As her hired car swept her through the Palace gates, she'd surely have remembered the reason she'd been invited. Perhaps the only remaining lady war veteran of the First World War, she'd have recalled wearing her Field Army Nurse's uniform and cranking her army ambulance before careening through the streets of Edinburgh at all of 25 miles per hour. Yes, I hope the Queen spared her a minute, with the few precious hours or days left for her—this gallant old lady of nearly 100.

A short while later, she had cataract surgery on both her eyes. During her recovery, it was my privilege to open, read and help her answer her letters. One of them always intrigued me, with beautiful writing and poetic wording flowing with loving phrases. One day I felt compelled to know more. "And who is this Donald who writes to you so regularly? Could it be that gentleman in the photograph on your wall?"

A blush and a nod confirmed my suspicions. "And how old is he, Mum?" I probed gently.

"Ninety-nine," she replied with a smile.

And so I felt like a modern Cyrano de Bergerac answering these letters as her amanuensis, a job that gave me the greatest pleasure. It slowly dawned on me that her reason for struggling to get to those First Great War veteran events was to see her Donald.

After her eye surgery, a nurse escorted her to France to commemorate the anniversary of the Battle of the Somme and meet the Duke of Gloucester. There, as the only woman among the remaining veterans, she joined a few old boys, one of whom was her beloved Donald. When she related the story to me, her eyes lit up when she spoke about seeing him there, along with another old flame, Michael, who had just celebrated his 103rd birthday. I can only imagine Mum's conversations with them, the fires still burning after so many years!

Though she was elderly and partly paralysed, she still enjoyed her private feelings and romantic dreams. Her philosophy of life was, "Never give up—never too old—another day, another experience." I'm sure there's something we can all learn from this brave soul!

CHAPTER 1

✈

My mother came from several generations of clergy and bishops, although her life was not particularly pious. In the First World War she trained as a mechanic in the Royal Army Service Corps, where her pay rose from 36 shillings a week to the princely sum of 42 shillings. She was then the only lady driver stationed to the north of Scotland, a somewhat tough assignment, as the lorries had no windscreens and had to be cranked by hand. Once trained, she trained other young girls to do the same work.

The job did have its compensations. Whilst driving some of the generals and brigadiers in the Glasgow riots, a truly frightening experience, she met Rupert Ernest Huntley-Flindt, a tall, dark, handsome staff captain. This romantic encounter resulted in their marriage in Edinburgh on St. Valentine's Day, secured by the Bishop of Edinburgh.

My father, who was a true Christian—quiet, humble and generous of spirit—was my mother's polar opposite. Every Sunday he would walk me up the narrow Devon lanes all of the three miles to church and at only five or six years old, I did my best to keep up with his long stride. During our walks, he helped shape my attitude toward helping others.

"Now, Chimp," he'd say, using a loving nickname he called me because I was so small and moved so quickly, "I'll give you 6 pence pocket money every week, but you must save 2p and give 2p to help someone less fortunate. The remaining 2p you can spend on yourself."

"Okay," I'd say, storing the information for later. I was usually much more interested in getting all the way to church so I could get my free bun. Someone had left an endowment to the church so the parishioners who attended would get free breakfast buns. At my young age, that was my Sunday goal!

On some of our walks, my father expounded on his philosophies on life, as with this quote he loved from Lao Zi (471 BC):

Hence the wise man depends on non-action for action,
Continues teaching his 'lessons of silence'
Yet the multitudinous creatures are influenced by him;
He does not reject them.

He nurtures them but claims no possession of them.
Accomplishes his purpose but does not dwell on his achievement.
And precisely because he calls no attention to his actions,
He is not banished from the completion of his tasks.

My father was my hero in life and I hung onto every word of advice and piece of knowledge he shared on those Sunday walks. I recall him vividly—a tall, elegant man with a quiet manner and great integrity whose own life reflected two of the greatest human virtues—humility and kindness. He taught by example how to be accepting rather than critical of others. When I lost this special man in 1966 to a heart attack, I lost my father and my mentor. I miss him to this day but am thankful for the sound advice he shared with me and my children.

My mother would go on to live a long and inspiring life, very much a presence in the lives of her children and grandchildren. In 1997, she died peacefully in her sleep at age 99. My sister Clare and I accepted her passing but were sorry that she hadn't reached 100. That would have brought her honors from the Queen, which she would have dearly loved.

✈

My parents first lived in Barnet where my brother, Michael Leighton, was born in 1922, followed a year later by me, christened Evette Huntley. Later we moved to Loddiswell, a sleepy village in the depths of South Devon, to a house called Higher Leigh. My father had left his international stock brokering firm in 1933, having saved enough to bring in £500 a year, which he felt would be sufficient to support us on an eight-acre apple and poultry farm. To be buried deep in the country proved a shattering blow to my mother, who was way ahead of her time, writing and lecturing on her pioneering theories on diet and health.

By 1933, when my mother became pregnant with her third child, my sister Rosemary Clare, there was no escape for her and she resigned herself to making the most of being a country housewife.

✈

As a child, I loved dancing, singing, dressing up and putting on little shows. I charged my friends and family tuppence each to come and watch, clearly showing early signs of entrepreneurship! The money was supposed to go to the next production but was frequently spent on sweets, which were forbidden by my mother.

When I was 10, I tried making money out of selling mustard and cress. I was already documenting my life in diaries and in one of the entries from that time, I wrote: "Lost 1 shilling on the packet, gained 7 shillings, having borrowed from the bank, gained 1 shilling and sixpence for a profit of 1 shilling and sixpence."

I also gave a little girl dancing lessons, charging a shilling and sixpence per class, but finding that not very profitable, I picked and sold my father's raspberries for 3 shillings and a half penny. My best gain from my odd jobs was from trapping rabbits; apart from thruppence for the loan of the trap, the gain was 10p!

THE WORLD WAS AT MY FEET

What brought my mother happiness was living vicariously through me. She was determined that I should become a ballet dancer and achieve more than just being educated at the local Kingsbridge School for Girls. So at 11, I was shipped off alone on the Paddington express train to London to be met by the head teacher of Heatherton House, a semi-dancing school that took promising young dancers. I was the happiest of all the boarders and after dull holidays in Devon, I couldn't wait to return to my school and dancing.

In my first year at Heatherton House, I won the school's dancing prize, a feat that clearly fired my mother's ambition for me. So the following year, she sent me off to the Cone School of Ballet in London where I stayed as a paying guest with the Fickling family, who had been friends of my parents. Their daughter, Brenda, became my great friend for life.

For the next few years, Brenda and I were inseparable and later, when the war started and food was in short supply, we would sit opposite each other in the bath with two spoons and a large, brown bottle of Radio Malt between us, discussing our ambitions and boyfriends until the water got cold. I could never have dreamed then that Brenda would become a prima ballerina— known by the name of Brenda Hamlyn—with the Rambert Ballet Company.

Because this was my mother's fondest wish for me too—to be a ballerina--she loved to hear about my dance training and other exploits. When my father went to war, serving as a major in the Royal Horse Artillery, stationed at Woolwich, she looked forward to receiving my weekly letters from London—they were the highlight of her week.

She was especially thrilled when I wrote and told her that I was going for my first important audition for a play by Marie Stopes called "Buckie's Bears," a professional production on the London stage. I'm not quite sure why she was so thrilled, as this was not a prestigious part. I would not be dancing; instead, I was to play the baby bear, covered from head to toe in white fur and charged with romping around the stage, playing practical jokes on the other more serious actors. It was a part I thoroughly enjoyed!

Meanwhile my mother made sure her other children also got a private boarding school education. My brother Michael was at Bryanstone School in Dorset and my sister Clare at Cranborne Chase School in Wimborne, both engaged in more scholarly pursuits than their theatrical sister. I admired them but was still drawn to what seemed like a more exciting life on stage.

I appeared in two more plays, Church Army "Sunbeams" and "The Boy Who Lost his Temper" and continued my training at ballet school, now called Cone-Ripman College (later known as Arts Educational School), where I gained honours in an Advanced Royal Academy Dance (RAD) course. Although the original Cone School had specialised in RAD technique, Ripman, the ballet school with which Cone had merged, specialised in the Cecchetti method. Regardless of their differences, both schools shared one ultimate goal: to develop prima ballerinas.

I loved dancing but even then I felt there was more to life than ballet; I was far too undisciplined and independent to be a professional dancer, much less a prima ballerina! I was more interested in mime, free dance and especially acting. My greatest ambition was to fit as many different experiences as I could into one life and I was determined never to get trapped in any job for too long.

The school had a theatrical agency attached to it, so students were notified of auditions for West End shows. Senior girls were constantly trotting off for auditions with their tights and point shoes packed in little hold-alls. Oh, those point shoes—how I hated them! I just didn't have the right feet. My big toes were far too long and actually creaked so much that my nickname at dance school was Creaky Toes Flindt.

I didn't mind, as I was having the time of my life; to me, wartime London was the most exciting place in the world. But my stay was cut short—as the war heated up, we were evacuated to the country where the Cone-Ripman School had rented a large, rambling mansion called The Hallams just outside Shamley Green. There we found ourselves not only distracted by the freedom of being away from home in the sunny countryside but also drawn to the old sweet shop in the middle of the village.

At that time my worldly experience was not very great. For the past several years I had been at ballet school in London where my basic education was rudimentary to say the least. Scholastic work there took second place to classical ballet, free dance, the piano, elocution, mime, tap and ballroom dancing. Still, they tried to educate me but I simply wasn't interested in academics. I'm ashamed to say I left school without a single scholastic qualification, and being dyslexic—a problem that had no diagnosis at the time—surely didn't help. It's something Richard inherited from me, but it never held either of us back.

Consequently my spelling has always been terrible and it is something of a family joke that I am Mrs Malaprop incarnate, forever using the wrong word or mixing my metaphors. Nevertheless, from a very early age, I had a vivid imagination and was always scribbling notes and writing articles, stories and plays. Nothing could get in the way of my lifelong passion for writing.

✈

I finished school at 17 but was still too young to join up for military service; with little employment to be found, I was hungry for work. So I was excited to present myself for an audition on a Tuesday morning in October 1941 at the London Palace Theatre, where I would dance for the world famous impresario, Sir Charles B. Cochran.

Mr Cochran was putting together a London revue called "Big Top" starring Beatrice Lillie and Fred Emney. He was looking for a new batch of attractive young dancers who would become known as Cochran's Young Ladies. His girls were chaperoned and he insisted on a high standard of personal behaviour. Although they were known for ending up quite scantily clad in some of their numbers, they were subject to dismissal if they married or were suspected of a sexual liaison!

It's hard to say what the modern equivalent of this corps of dancers would be. They were somewhere between the Tiller Girls and Pan's People, though nowhere near as racy as the Windmill showgirls. At any rate, Mr Cochran's Young Ladies were hugely glamorous and the star-struck Evette Huntley-Flindt longed to be one of them.

Looking back, I think the word "giddy" was invented especially for me, as that described me perfectly at that time in my life. I thought I was going to live forever. Thus, when the day of my audition to be a Cochran's Young Lady arrived, I hadn't given a single thought to what I was going to perform. I simply turned up at the Palace Theatre expecting nothing and having prepared nothing at all. At least I was there on time. In fact, I was an hour early, which gave me a chance to watch all the other young hopefuls going through their paces.

They all seemed terrifyingly polished and professional to me. Standing there in the wings, I watched one after another executing a perfect performance—just what had I let myself in for? I got more and more depressed as I watched. In fact I was about to turn tail and run when my name was called. With the lights full on me, there was nothing to do but to step forward.

Miss Prim, the pianist, was a rather formal woman in her late fifties who had been playing for Mr Cochran for years and had developed a theatrical way of striking the chords, raising her wrists high and ending pieces with a dramatic flourish. Her face, framed with severe horn-rimmed spectacles, expressed a mixture of horror and disdain when I told her that not only did I have no music with me but I hadn't even prepared a dance piece for my audition. Would she mind awfully just playing whatever she thought suitable and I would mime something?

Forever living for the present, all I could think of to mime was a young girl going to an audition and discovering she was performing before a live audience and hadn't prepared a thing! With a chair for a prop, I sat down in the middle of the stage and went through the motions of watching the curtains part and then realising to my great distress that there was a full house out there.

Miss Prim did her best. She must have felt sorry for me because she managed to keep up with my improvisations. She played suitable music to take me through a series of emotions that were not too far from reality—fear, worry and panic, which turned into a sort of manic whirling abandon.

After six or seven pirouettes, I returned to my chair and shrugged my shoulders as the curtains closed. Then, overwhelmed by what I had done, I ran off the stage, fighting back the tears. It took me a few moments to decipher the noise I heard on the other side of the curtains, which seemed to be laughter and clapping. I was convinced that I had made a complete fool of myself, so imagine my surprise and delight when two weeks later I received a card from Mr Cochran's secretary, Miss Florence Peters, telling me that I got the job. I was going to be one of Mr Cochran's Young Ladies! I was beside myself with joy and celebrated by having a lemonade shandy with my dancing friends.

I longed to break the news to my father at the Woolwich Barracks. Every Sunday afternoon he would meet me at the Grosvenor Hotel in Park Lane, where they held a weekly tea dance, and attempt to check up on my welfare. Hoping to safeguard his daughter's virginity, he would encourage me to choose a shandy over a stronger gin and lime. On the Sunday before the audition, we had met as usual and I admit that I was somewhat economical regarding the truth when I described the dances Mr Cochran's Young Ladies were required to do. I told my father that "it wasn't quite classical ballet" but I didn't elaborate further.

Major Rupert Huntley-Flindt was not one to be deceived by his 17-year-old flibbertigibbet of a daughter. He made his own enquiries and by the time I rang to give him my marvellous news, he had already decided that Mr Cochran—the man responsible for most of the major West End hits of the day and a personal friend of Noel Coward—was going to have to manage without me.

My father did have a point. As it happened, the dance that I was supposed to perform five nights a week on a West End stage was about clothes rationing. It was called "Coupon Striptease" and it ended up with the Young Ladies prancing about the stage in little more than dusters!

So my joyous telephone call ended in gloom. My father told me firmly that under no circumstance was I going to be seen flitting across the West End stage, scantily clad. To my dismay and horror, he said he would contact Mr Cochran and that is exactly what he did, undoubtedly in his most charming and diplomatic way. I was distraught; my dreams of becoming a Cochran Young Lady were shattered.

I never knew exactly what was said but incredibly, Mr Cochran, then a man in his late 50's, assured my father that his daughter would not have to take her clothes off. A kindly man despite his fame, he was as good as his word. I was to present myself at the Palace Theatre once again and bring my practice clothes. I still have the card, sent from Mr Cochran's Old Bond Street office, where the address for telegrams was "Cockranus, Piccy, London" and the telephone number was "Regent 0424."

I arrived at the theatre in a very agitated state. I was ushered in to see the great man himself. "Sit down, young lady. I have been speaking to your father and I understand his misgivings, so we are not going to employ you as one of the Mr Cochran's Young Ladies. Your audition was so good, however, that we are going to give you an acting part instead. You can tell your father," he said with a twinkle, "that you don't have to take your clothes off!"

Well, you could hardly call it an acting part. It involved dressing up in a glamorous gown and pretending to be enjoying myself in a box at the opera. Nevertheless I was thrilled to be part of a major West End show. My role called for me to sit in box number five with my "date" for the evening—Fred Emney himself. Beatrice Lillie sat in box number four with another actress.

I proudly sent a copy of the programme to my mother in Devon with my stage name—Evette Huntley—underneath Fred Emney's. Though just over 40 at the time, he seemed quite old to me. Even in those days he had acquired his signature monocle, which he must have had difficulty keeping in place because he appeared to be constantly winking at me. This embarrassed me terribly whenever he looked my way until I realised it was just a nervous twitch.

SIRENS, BOMBS, AND DOODLEBUGS

The war was now gathering momentum with frequent air raid sirens, bombs, and doodlebugs raining down on London. A note at the foot of the each theatre programme advised theatregoers that in the event of an air raid warning, an announcement would be made from the stage. Patrons were advised to remain in the theatre although they could also go to the nearest air raid shelter if they wished.

I can't remember that ever happening during a performance. Theatre folk seemed determined that the show would go on despite the efforts of Mr Hitler, although I do remember scurrying to the theatre one day with doodlebugs falling from the skies, setting fire to nearby buildings.

My first pay packet contained all of £5 for a week's work. I thought that was a fortune and I celebrated with a shandy in a pub around the corner from the theatre. Women never paid for their own drinks in wartime London and that day, I was so elated that I didn't keep a close eye on my handbag. It was only when it was time to leave that I discovered to my deep dismay that my very first pay packet had been stolen. I was upset, but even then I didn't believe in crying over spilt milk, so I vowed never to let my handbag out of my sight again.

That wasn't the end of the sad story, however, as two days later I received an anonymous letter asking me to meet a Mr Jones in Hyde Park by the second tree on the left after the arch, as he wished to return my bag! I duly let the police know, thrilled at the chance of a real drama. Detective Inspector Eve Flindt was going to catch the thief and the police had assured me they would be standing by. I was filled with excitement until I told my father, who responded in no uncertain terms that I was not to proceed with this risky plan. Instead he would reimburse my £5 himself.

✈

In 1942 I appeared in "Big Top" at His Majesty's Theatre, with sets designed by Oliver Messel and a script written by Herbert Farjeon. The dramatic critic for the *Daily Telegraph* wrote: "Loveliness and liveliness in generous combination are frequently and abundantly bestowed and there is hardly a scene in the show which does not glow with the one or sparkle with the other."

Along with praise for the "cool sparkle" of the actress and comedic performer Beatrice Lillie, and more important to me and my friends, was a line about us: "Mr Cochran's Young Ladies, a most attractive and gifted bevy of many types of beauty, decorate the stage and the music includes some tunes that should remain popular for years to come."

By today's politically correct standards, those words might seem patronising, but in those days we thought they were quite wonderful. The review was quickly dispatched to my mother in Devon where it was lovingly filed along with other newspaper clippings about my career.

At the time I was in awe of Beatrice Lillie. I would watch and admire her and silently respect her fame from afar, feeling much too timid to actually talk to her. I couldn't help wondering if I too would ever become a famous lady of the stage.

Another cutting my mother collected was from the *Yorkshire Evening News*. It shows a line-up of seven of Cochran's Young Ladies photographed in Leeds where we were making a personal appearance. Before the shows intended for London were performed, they would test them out on suburban audiences, which meant the cast would travel around to the English counties. Often the digs were somewhat squalid but we didn't mind, as the performance each night was all that mattered to us; the excitement of being on stage was enough.

Another show I remember well was George Black's "Strike a New Note". The lead was Zoe Gail, a stunning redhead, who did a wonderful number, "I'm Going to Get Lit Up," written by the incomparable Hubert Gregg, who also wrote the hit song, "Maybe It's Because I'm a Londoner" after watching German doodlebug missiles fly over his London home.

Dressed in top hat and tails, the beautiful Zoe was supposed to be a man-about-town telling us what he was going to do when the blackouts ceased and the lights went on in London once more. It brought the house down every time. This was a spoof on a famous radio reporter who, whilst under the influence and slurring his words, reported over the airwaves that the fleets were "getting lit up"!

CHAPTER 1

Zoe's only son was in the army and one day, halfway through the run at the Prince of Wales Theatre, a telegram arrived to say that he had been killed. Unbelievably, in true theatre tradition, Zoe went on stage that night as if nothing had happened. I have never forgotten that heartbreaking show of professionalism.

✈

My first wartime love was John Raper, a fighter pilot I met through a friend in the theatre. When he was on leave, we'd dress up and go to London to The Milroy Nightclub or the 400 Club and dance the night away. In those days we danced what we called the "good night shuffle". We would start by holding our partner in a waltz position and slowly walk round and round. But as the music got more romantic, we would capture the mood and tighten our embrace. By the time the music ended, the room was filled with couples holding each other tight, barely moving. Toward the end of each dance I would start to feel sad, wondering if I would be able to hold on to my beloved John or whether the war would destroy our precious friendship.

When he was sent out on dangerous night flights over Germany, I always worried that he would not return. All my girlfriends lived with the same fear day after day, which is why our evenings at the night clubs were so special and romantic for all of us.

When I kissed John goodbye after one of his leaves, I didn't know that would be the last time I'd see him. Day after day would go by as I waited for news. I never did learn what happened to John but I'm certain he was killed in action, like so many of our brave young men.

✈

By 1943 I was earning the great sum of £7 for a week's work in the theatre. Some of my roles were serious but others had an impish twist, which matched the nickname "Chimp" my father had so endearingly called me as a child.

Amongst the dancers I worked with in "Strike a New Note" were two young men with whom I became quite friendly. Eric Morecambe and Ernie Wise were ordinary hoofers like the rest of us, but they were just beginning to put together what would become their famous comic double act known as Morecambe & Wise. Eric never could resist the opportunity to entertain an audience. We would sit backstage or at the pub after the show and roar with laughter at their improvisations and mimicry.

My final foray on the West End stage was in Sir Alan Herbert's "Bless the Bride". I understudied for four of the sisters' roles and the role of the pageboy, Buttons, which was played by a little West Indian boy. As an understudy I was paid an extra 10 shillings a week, but sadly I never got to appear in any of the performances. I was rather relieved that the little boy in the play was never ill, as I would have been required to darken my skin with stage make-up and wear a black wig to hide my blonde hair. I did love some of the tunes in that show including "I Was Never Kissed Before" and "Ma Belle Marguerite," which later became popular songs.

Every evening I turned up at the theatre in plenty of time, only to be told that everyone was fighting fit and I would not be needed. So I would go to the foyer bar where author Sir Alan Herbert held court. His tales of past theatrical triumphs were fascinating and he was clearly happy to have such an attentive audience. Hearing him talk about his novels and plays sparked a longing in me to be a well-known writer someday too.

About this time the painter Sir Russell Flint did some sketches of the cast, one of which is hanging in my bathroom at our home in West Sussex. It's a little faded but I'm there all right, clearly recognizable. I'm posing at the far right of the other girls, dressed in a frilly maid's costume, complete with a white headpiece and lacy apron, with one arm outstretched and the other holding up a tray of empty wine glasses. It is a wonderful souvenir of my dancing years. Whilst the great man painted, he filled his wastepaper basket with discarded sketches. I remember thinking how I would like to take that wastepaper basket home!

✈

With no home in London, I first stayed in a "ladies club" at Lancaster Gate because my parents thought it would keep me out of trouble. About 40 young women slept in a vast dormitory with curtains around the beds. Everybody took a turn at fire-watch duty on the roof; we would have to stay up there alone for two hours at a time, cold and silent. When it was my turn, I was not only cold but terrified, seeing the searchlight flashing hither and thither, looking for any signs of doodlebugs landing nearby. The loos were located in the depths of the basement, which gave me the excuse to spend a lot of pennies during my watch.

Later I moved into Manson Mews, a lovely little cottage in West London, with my friend Pru James, who had been dancing in another show whilst I was the understudy in "Bless the Bride". To help pay the rent, we found a tenant, John George Haigh, to live in the flat below us. He always seemed to be amused at the way Pru and I lived. We really felt we'd arrived and were proud to bring our friends back to our charming flat. All was rosy until one day there was a knock on our door. It was the police asking politely whether a John George Haigh kept his car in the garage below. Yes, we said, shocked to learn from the police that our tenant was a notorious murderer who disposed of his victims in an acid bath! Only when he was safely behind bars were we able to go back to enjoying our mews house and concentrate again on our dancing careers and boyfriends.

FLYING SOLO

It was a bittersweet time for me, as it was for many young single women surrounded by handsome servicemen who were constantly in danger. How well I remember one wonderful Army Guards officer, Michael Hargraves, the man I thought I'd marry—it was truly love at first sight. He was an even more serious love interest than my former boyfriend John. We exchanged love letters when he was away and talked about marriage when we were together. I was close to his parents too, who had all three of their sons in the war, Michael being the eldest.

One terrible day I received the dreaded telegram saying Michael had been killed in active service. I was devastated. And I soon learned that my last long love letter to him was returned to my mother's address, unopened. I never got over that. Later I learned that both his brothers were also killed in the line of duty—what a sacrifice that family made for their country!

Although it was exciting to be in the theatre, I was tiring of life on the stage and wanted to contribute to the war effort myself, so I began to think about how to end my theatrical career. I didn't imagine it would be a difficult transition because I was only an understudy. Despite having signed up for the run of a successful show, I invented a heart problem and suggested that the doctors were not very happy with me working such late hours. The producers accepted my reason for leaving and I moved on to a new career.

At just that time, somebody told me that the Air Training Corps were looking for help training cadets to fly gliders. They only wanted men for this job, however, so I decided to disguise myself as best I could in men's clothing, skip my morning dance class and turn up at the glider training centre at Heston, Middlesex.

There were more than a few astonished looks when I strolled across the airfield to inquire whether I could train to become a glider pilot. I was asked whether I had any experience, which of course I hadn't, but I explained that I would love to learn and help out in any way I could. The officer in charge agreed to take me on as an "Instructor under Instruction," providing that I kept pretending to be a boy (I guess my disguise fell a little short). Headquarters certainly wouldn't sanction a woman in such a dangerous sport.

My life soon revolved around wonderful weekends at Heston, giving last-minute instructions to the young boys before they soared into the air. My only worry at the time was walking the length of the airfield with all eyes upon me when I had to visit the so-called Ladies! First I was taught how to work the winch, after which I was instructed in ground slides, an essential discipline before being allowed to take off. In spite of the gender restriction, it wasn't long before I was allowed to fly solo. (All the gliders were single seaters in those days, so there was no opportunity to fly with an instructor.)

For my first flight I was winched 300 feet into the air, flying in a closed pattern—downwind, base, and final legs—the cadets and officers watching with pride below. As I soared higher and higher, I took fright when I looked down. Forgetting the vital instructions I had given other pilots, I inadvertently released the nose from the winch cable whilst the nose was pointing skyward, stalling the glider. In a panic I pulled the release lever and the glider spiralled towards the ground at an ever-increasing speed. In my twirling descent I felt sick and dizzy. Then out of the corner of my eye, I noticed the famous Brabberson prototype plane, worth millions, sitting peacefully at one end of the airfield. I was headed straight towards it!

Thankfully, a calm, inner resolve took hold of me just in time and I pulled the stick back, landing gently alongside the Brabberson. I stepped out of the glider, shaking, and was met by an ashen-faced crowd of officers and cadets who had run across the airfield to greet me. They insisted—quite rightly—that I do it again. This time, which would be my second and final glider flight, I remembered my instructions: never, ever release from the winch when the nose of the glider is facing upwards to the sky. And perhaps another lesson learnt: leave gliding to the boys. (Sorry, girls!)

MORSE CODE AND MTBS

In 1943, when the war was in its fourth year, I was 19 and finally old enough to join up. Every girl wanted to become a WREN—a member of the Women's Royal Naval Service--could it have been partly the uniform? So I found out where the London recruiting office was situated and brazenly walked in to announce that I should like become a WREN, adding that I would like to work in the open and preferably with ships. I was fascinated by the sea, which seemed to me mysterious, romantic and exciting too. My pure audacity must have done the trick, as they offered me a job as a visual signaller right there on the spot.

Visual signallers were known as "Bunting Tossers". To communicate, we were instructed in the Morse code with hand-held Aldis lamps or with the 10-inch lamp or semaphore with flags for ships farther away. Today's technology has made such signalling outdated, but in those days it was an effective means of communication.

Within a few weeks I was issued my uniform—bell-bottom trousers and a saucy little hat—and was sent to Warrington, Lancaster, an inland country town, along with hundreds of other women and sailors for signal training. I have no idea why I was chosen for this job when I couldn't even spell. But four months later, eight of us were posted to the Black Isle in Scotland where most of the invasion fleet was based.

Our first night on watch was absolute agony; lights were flashing from every direction and none of us could understand a word, let alone a letter! We all felt responsible and believed the war would be lost if we could not read their messages. We gradually got the hang of it, however, and were soon flashing responses and other messages to the officers and ratings in the bay.

Before long the bay was teeming with ships on exercise, prior to going south for the main invasion of the war. Tension was rising and we were no longer granted shore leave; there was time only to sleep, eat and signal. One afternoon all the ships left the Basin and only then did we realise that the invasion was imminent.

As the majority of ships had left Scotland and gone south, our next posting was Yarmouth, the Isle of Wight. The island bristled with activity, every spare corner teeming with servicemen; no civilians were allowed to enter or leave the island without special permission. The seven other signalling WRENs were billeted with me above the local chemist shop.

There was no danger of putting on weight, as our food rations were limited—we had no meat, fish or eggs. But there was a pub nearby called the Folly Inn whose owner either felt sorry for us or perhaps found us reasonably attractive in our uniforms. Whenever we went for drinks, he somehow managed to find a boiled egg for each of us!

I'm almost ashamed to say that my year in the quaint village of Yarmouth was one of the best in my life. The other seven WRENs and I bonded very closely. Wandering down the pier, night or day, was no hardship, nor was standing outside in all kinds of weather, flashing to the many ships in the Solent. Wrapped in a duffel coat, with cocoa always on the boil in our little hut at the end of the pier on an island swarming with young, attractive servicemen—what more could an unattached young WREN possibly want?

One night I was having trouble reading a ship's Morse code flashing at us in our little round hut when a sailor in a dinghy tied up at our jetty. "Little WREN," he said, "It seems you're having trouble with your Morse code. I will teach you a secret, and I guarantee you'll never forget it." He took my message pad and proceeded to write the alphabet in capitals upon which he pressed harder over each letter, demonstrating the dots and dashes: A •−, B −•••, C −•−• and so on. As he did so, I was able to visualize the shape of each letter according the dots and dashes in the code. Magic! After five minutes I was flashing away messages with my lamps to the passing ships in half the time.

When each ship passed, we had to take note of their call sign so we could document their safe return, but most often we were communicating with motor torpedo boats (MTBs) and motor launchers (MLs), speedy vessels that would dash into the fjords of Norway, fire their torpedoes and get the hell back to safety.

Life at the end of that pier was not only exciting but romantic too. I recall one cold night in December when the moon was full and there was no movement from the ships. Bundled in my duffel coat, I peered through our telescope and my gaze fell upon a handsome Lieutenant Commander dressed in a warm white naval jersey on one of the MTBs. I quickly dashed off a message with my lamp, but I was unable to understand his reply, so I sent the message again, more slowly: "Would you come alongside?" Such an unlikely message did the trick and immediately he brought his ship up to our pier. That night the watch passed more quickly than usual as we sipped hot cocoa and talked. As he was leaving, I admired his cosy white jersey, which had caught my eye through the lens of the telescope.

You can imagine my joy and surprise when the next day, a large brown parcel arrived, addressed to the blonde WREN on watch the previous night, and on opening it, I found a gloriously warm white naval jersey! But the story does not end there, as that gift was the beginning of a wonderful romance. Whenever my Lieutenant Commander returned to the island, we would take long walks until late, when we would sleep on the beach under the stars or in the forest nearby. It was an exciting but stressful relationship, as I never knew whether he'd return from his next trip to France. Eventually I lost touch with him, but the joy of that romance stayed with me well beyond the end of the war. More than 50 years later, I was able to relive those exciting days when I found that the very same MTB I had signalled from still existed. Miraculously, it was moored in the harbour only minutes from my home.

✈

In May 2000, whilst strolling down the peaceful harbour of Chichester, I noticed what at first glance looked like just another houseboat. An old, scruffy wooden craft, it had clearly seen better days and looked rather out of place among the shiny modern fibreglass boats moored along a peaceful stretch of the canal. It would have been easy to amble on, lost in the bucolic beauty of the place, but something about this particular boat drew my attention away from the quacking ducks, the regal swans swimming against the tide and the moorhens burrowing in the rushes.

It might have been the faded paintwork, with patches of battle grey showing through in places, or the incongruously sleek, rakish lines of her wooden hull that brought back poignant memories from my days as a young WREN on Yarmouth Pier. Could it be the same little craft, I wondered, that I had signalled on that bitterly cold winter night?

My wistful reminiscing was interrupted by a voice that cut through the summer haze. "Ahoy, there, like to come aboard?" the handsome man on deck shouted. I crossed the rickety gangplank and was thrilled to find the owner, David Watson, a racing driver and stunt man fascinated with old cars and boats, who was busily renovating, yes, my old MTB! He was too young to have been in the war, but he recounted the fascinating story of how the past owner had transformed it from a wartime torpedo boat into a houseboat, keeping all of the original screws and other hardware hidden behind the skirting boards!

On the owner's death, the MTB was bequeathed to David on the condition that he restore it to its original condition. Thus it was that when David was working on it, he was startled to find wodges of notes and beautiful jewellery hidden behind pieces of panelling as he pried them off. It was not only a historic boat but a treasure trove too! He was lucky also to discover that the previous owner had carried out only basic modifications, making it possible to restore the plucky little craft to her original state. David was confident that when the restoration was completed, his MTB-71 would one day lie next to HMS *Victory*, HMS *Warrior*, and the *Mary Rose* as the fourth wooden fighting ship representing Britain's naval heritage.

Noting my great interest and curiosity, David invited me below. I made the hazardous descent down a makeshift ladder, groping my way in the dark empty hull, tripping over loose floorboards and knocking my head on the low bulkhead. When I struggled back up the ladder to the wheelhouse, still festooned with old flowerpots and hanging baskets, David recounted the history of the MTB-71. Built in 1937, it was one of the British Navy's affectionately regarded "little ships" that fought with distinction in more than 780 actions. The brave fighting men on board these ships, who numbered 22,000 by 1944, were responsible for sinking 800 enemy vessels, including 48 MTBs and 43 mini-submarines.

It was said that the average age of the MTB crew members was 20 and their wooden crafts were little more than floating bombs, packed as they were with 1,000 gallons of highly flammable high-octane petrol, along with torpedo and depth charges. Their only defence was speed.

Memories flooded back, overwhelming me. The minute I got home that day, I scrambled into the loft to find my old Aldis lamp. It was dusty and a bit rusty but otherwise in good working order. As I held it up in the darkness, I found myself transported back to that icy evening during the war when the face of that handsome MTB officer came into focus through my telescope.

I later gave my lamp to David as a present to put inside the MTB-71, thinking perhaps someone somewhere would see this out-of-date lamp, polished and glistening, and might send a new white naval jersey to the little old lady who is now sorely in need of a re-fit herself!

THE BALLERINA IN BELL-BOTTOMS

It was 1945 and with the war over and a pittance to live on, I decided to contact my old ballet friend, Brenda, who had persevered through the war with the Ballet Rambert. Brenda was about to tour Germany with the company under the supervision of the Entertainments National Services Association (ENSA). "Why don't you come too?" she suggested.

The idea was outrageous and ridiculous. I was so out of practice, I even groaned at the thought of a plié!

"Where's your spirit, Eve?" she complained.

I immediately rang Madam Rambert's secretary, made an appointment for an audition and donned my bell-bottom trousers.

(I had no coupons left to buy any tights.) Brenda had lent me a pair of her point-shoes, so off I went.

Fortunately, Mim—as Madame Rambert was known—had a sense of humour, scarcely believing what she saw—a ballerina in bell-bottom trousers prancing around the stage. Fortunately, she decided to take me on as a member of the corps de ballet. "At least you will keep the troops amused, if nothing else," she muttered under her breath. I was ecstatic but sure she would come to regret accepting me. Meanwhile, Brenda had watched from the wings, laughing herself silly on seeing me in my baggy trousers and worn-out point-shoes with dirty pink laces that she must have retrieved from the attic!

I was 21 years old, nervous and excited about what lay ahead! Swapping my blue WRENs uniform for a khaki ENSA outfit, I hastened off to join Brenda at Victoria Station on a cold, foggy morning. The entire cast of dancers including the prima ballerina, Sally Gilmour, were all wearing identical uniforms. The purpose of the tour was simple: we were charged under the British Army Welfare with entertaining the 30th Corps British troops in Germany. I had my doubts about whether they would find classical ballet to their liking, but we were certainly intent on showing our appreciation to them.

We left Folkestone in thick fog with the entire ballet company and 500 troops on board the Royal Seagull. Accommodations below deck were pretty uncomfortable. It was dark and cold hour upon hour, with no food or drink, and all we heard was the rhythmical groan of the foghorn. Those who went above deck tried to keep warm by huddling beneath benches and underneath duffel coats in the bottom of the lifeboats.

In desperation, I persuaded Brenda to come up to the bridge with me to talk to the captain. He was charming and allowed us to use his cabin, a luxury indeed, although conversation was difficult as he spoke only Belgian. He must have felt sorry for us shivering young dancers, for he sent a steward up with tea, toast and sandwiches, followed by the generous offer to help ourselves to his gin.

With the fog thickening, our boat became stranded outside Calais, and there was little food left on board, so the captain sent one of the lifeboats ashore asking for immediate provisions. But after a few hours, the fog had thickened and when the lifeboat did not return, the captain looked seriously worried because we needed to make contact with the shore. I asked him if I might help by using his 10-inch signal lamp, which I believed would penetrate the fog.

Climbing onto the bridge, I first shined it over the water for any sign of the lifeboat before sending a message ashore to the Calais signal station. To my surprise, I deciphered a return message that the lifeboat was still ashore but a tugboat would shortly bring food and provisions.

This brought a bit of praise in the form of another glass of gin, along with a welcome invitation to spend the night in the captain's cabin. By now Brenda and I were frozen and glad to accept, leaving the ballerinas and the 500 troops strewn all over the rest of the ship, doing their best to keep warm.

The tug and lifeboats finally arrived the next day when the fog lifted, and soon after we were able to sail into Calais harbour. There we boarded buses and drove to Ostend to embark on a grim 30-hour train journey to Hamburg, having to sit up all night with blacked-out windows and no heat. But we accepted our small share of hardship, knowing we were there for a good cause.

Our next two months entertaining the troops in Germany were a mixture of heaven and hell. We spent a week in each bomb-shattered town—Lubeck, Flensburg, Brunswick, Celle, Berlin and Brussels—rehearsing during the day and dancing in any of the still existing theatres at night. We knew the troops were starved for good entertainment, as they seemed to enjoy our repertoire of ballets, including Swan Lake, Les Sylphides, and Giselle.

It was a strange time. It was fun when we were being chatted up by the troops but disconcerting when we interacted with the Germans. We tried to be cordial but it wasn't easy. Some Germans were eager to talk, telling us of their hatred for the Nazis; others kept their distance.

Some of our experiences in the German towns were chilling. I remember being in Lubeck, a former Nazi stronghold, where children spat at us in the streets, and seeing the carnage in Münster, where a handful of soulless people shuffled through the rubble, looking for scraps of food.

The weather was bitterly cold, with lots of ice and snow, and our accommodations rarely provided much comfort. I remember that Sally, our lead dancer, had to sleep in an attic with the only loo situated two floors below.

I have one lovely memory from those days. Just outside Berlin, a young, handsome British General invited me to go riding with him and lent me a thoroughbred Army horse. We went galloping through the forest, playing hide-and-seek as we wove in and out through the trees. It was thrilling but perhaps a bit risky for a working ballet dancer!

When my contract was over and my khaki uniform turned in, I'm sure Madam Rambert was thankful she would no longer need to watch from the stalls as Eve Huntley struggled to perform with her bloodied point-shoes and arabesques that were half as high as the others.

But what next, I thought. I had thrown myself into the war effort, but what would the future hold for me? I was young and ambitious but untrained for the civilian life that lay ahead. I did, however, have my war gratuity, the princely sum of £21.40!

✈

Whilst I was cavorting about, my more serious brother, Michael, 18 months my senior, qualified as a doctor and held the post as house physician and senior casualty officer at St. Helier Hospital before being appointed as the resident anaesthetist and house surgeon at St. Thomas Hospital in London. In 1947 he married a St. Thomas nurse, Mary Pruen Sloper, and eventually they had three children. His next appointment was in Borneo where he was in charge of a 100-bed hospital, finding himself alone and responsible for all the operations. It wasn't all work, however, for he managed to have a golf handicap in single figures and played tennis in a Davis Cup tournament.

In his retirement, he painted and played the clarinet in an orchestra. With MB, BS, FFOM, DIH, LRCP, and MRCS after his name, I've always felt proud to call him my brother, and relieved to realise that there was one of us, at least, who was focused on a serious career!

Meanwhile my younger sister Clare became an entrepreneur in her own right. After she married, she went to live in a Norfolk mill house on a small farm and became obsessed with Welsh mountain sheep, which she finally managed to bring off the endangered species list. She organised a thriving business called The Black Sheep Marketing Company, having trained as a shepherdess, and had all the old ladies in the village knitting the black wool into mittens, shawls, and sweaters.

Years later, when Richard was being honoured by the *This Is Your Life* programme, Clare brought ten of her black sheep from Norfolk to the BBC-TV studio in London, somewhat to the surprise of those Londoners who caught sight of the animals trotting happily down Bond Street! That day, Richard recorded the song "BaaBaa Black Sheep," which included the sounds of Clare's sheep, ducks and hens in the chorus. Who would have believed that it would become a hit single on Top of the Pops?

One of Clare's closest friends was Douglas Bader, a World War II ace pilot who lost both legs in a near-fatal plane crash. After Clare earned her flying licence, they bought a small bi-plane that gave them many scary moments, much to the anxiety of her husband, Gerard Hoare, who was patiently minding her sheep at home. Like me, Clare loved risk and adventure. Letters back home to our parents must have given them some hair-raising concern, though I'm sure my mother felt a tinge of jealousy as she read about our escapades!

CHAPTER 2

AFTER THE WAR, GREAT BRITAIN was a dreary place. Food rationing was strict; our meagre daily ration was a mouthful of butter, meat, cheese and offal, with only one egg a week and no citrus fruit. We filled in with vegetables, which everyone grew in their back gardens as best they could. How we craved meat from the butcher, though!

Desperate to get out of England and see the world, what better, I thought, than to become an air hostess and travel to exotic countries? Little did I realise there was at least a year's waiting list for young women anxious to trade post-war deprivation for glamour in the air.

Never daunted, I found the recruitment centre and chatted up the doorman, who told me about British South American Airways (BSAA), a new airline scheduled to fly between London and South America. It was privately owned by Wing Commander Don Bennett, an ex-RAF pathfinder and later founder and chairman of the United Nations Association.

The kindly, pot-bellied doorman, his eyes twinkling above his well-manicured moustache, told me that to qualify as an air hostess, one needed to be between 23 and 27 years old, under 6 feet 4 inches tall and unmarried. Candidates would also need to have some nursing experience. After a pause, and with a wink, he added that it was necessary to be a virgin and speak at least two other languages. Well, at least I was 24 years old, of average height and unmarried!

Terribly nervous, I arrived at the recruitment centre to join 30 other anxious young girls in the waiting room. Tentatively I peeked over my newspaper. They all looked so very much more beautiful and obviously much more efficient than I could ever be. One by one we were called until my turn finally came. May God forgive me for not answering their questions entirely truthfully. Yes, I could speak two languages and, yes, I had nurse's training. They did seem to be quite impressed when I told them I had trained to be a glider pilot. I purposely left out the details! With questions over, they said they would let me know in a week or so. In my fluster I bowed out, only to take the wrong door and find myself in the broom cupboard—not a good start! So you can imagine my surprise and delight when the acceptance letter arrived a week later.

How well I remember 16 February 1947 when I had to give up my last precious wartime clothes coupons for a saucy little cap and blue, tailored uniform created by Norman Hartnell, the famous designer. It was meant to enhance the figure with a short, tight skirt and silk stockings with a seam down the back, all considered very sexy in those days. The shoes were flat and sturdy. Little did I know they were designed to accommodate many hours of standing on the job.

Our various short training courses included a lesson on a grounded horse-glider (once used to fly paratroopers to Arnhem, Netherlands during the war) that had been converted to resemble the interior of a passenger plane. It was on this plane that we learned the ditching drill—how I enjoyed sliding down that shoot!

Another course was at Cadby Hall, where Andy, the chief chef, an amusing, well-fed Cockney, was supposed to teach us how to garnish sandwiches. Most of the time he regaled us with his experiences about the goings-on at the various private houses where he'd worked, such as that of the Duke and Duchess of Windsor. He recounted being given the job of teaching Billy Butlin—the originator of cheap holiday camps for the masses—how to be a gentleman. We ended our week at Cadby Hall, if no wiser on matters of catering, certainly more enlightened as to the chef's attitude toward life.

At the time, BSAA had two types of planes in operation: 13-passenger Lancastrians and 21-passenger, four-engine Yorks with names like Star Stream and Star Dale. Thus we air hostesses were known as Star Girls. The flight crews consisted of a captain, first officer, navigator and radio officer, all of whom had recently retired from the Royal Air Force.

The day finally arrived when we had to report for duty. I was feeling fine until the day of my maiden flight on Star Stream, when my courage threatened to fail me. It was a cold morning. Nervous and shivering, I waited for the crew van to pick me up outside Kensington Underground Station and drive me to London Airport to meet the other Star Girls and crew.

In a small Nissen hut at Heathrow Airport, we were given our pay packets (all of £5 and 10 shillings) and our itineraries for the flight route from London to Santiago, Chile. It would take 20 days and require six stopovers for refuelling and three crew changes. The experienced Star Girls told me our first priority was to get rid of the "No Tipping" notice in the cabin, so I found that a screwdriver was to be an essential tool for this job!

In trepidation I boarded the York aircraft to meet my 18 passengers. First I collected the passenger list and then handed around chewing gum and barley sugar, which we told passengers to chew to stop their ears from bursting. I also passed out cotton wool they could use to drown out the loud engine noise and Penguin books to keep them occupied during the flight. I then explained delicately that all passengers should swallow and blow their noses in preparation for take-off and landing to avoid burst eardrums. I told them about the emergency and ditching instructions and pointed out the sick bags in the pockets at the back of each passenger's seat; these invariably proved essential. Finally I made sure they were strapped in and, if we were lucky, we Star Girls would find an empty seat for takeoff.

If there were no seats available, we had to sit on "diplomatic bags," large sacks, secured by a lock and chain, that had been carried on board by an embassy official. I assumed these bags contained secret messages being ferried between the UK and South American embassies.

My first flight as a Star Girl left England on 26 March 1947 at 0905 hours. I was excited and afraid as our speed increased until we were racing at 100 miles per hour down the runway. We climbed into the air, jerking and bumping until we reached the cruising height of 10,000 feet, with an air speed of approximately 25 knots. We were on our way!

✈

A five-hour flight took us to our first destination, Portella Airport in Lisbon, for fuel refill and breakfast, a meal to be remembered. We feasted on bacon, eggs, butter and marmalade, such as we'd not seen for five long years. Oh, the thrill—and later, the indigestion and stomach cramps—but it was worth it!

The only two passengers to board at Lisbon were the Armenian petroleum tycoon Nubar Gulbenkian and his valet, who not only brought their own picnic hamper but also tipped the Star Girls the vast sum of a pound each. They were welcome passengers indeed!

When we re-boarded for our next leg, I was beginning to feel somewhat more confident but this proved premature, as we hit frequent storms during the gruelling eight-hour flight to Dakar, the capital of Senegal, West Africa. The turbulence, noise and lack of pressurisation in the cabin were not only uncomfortable but alarming too. However, we did our best to reassure our passengers that all was well, despite feeling sick ourselves. Adding to our nausea was the pungent smell of Jeyes Fluid toilet cleanser that filled our nostrils as we passed back and forth through the cabin. With my stomach turning and my ankles swelling, those eight hours felt like they would never end.

Finally we arrived at Dakar, where we were scheduled to take a much-needed rest. Peering out from the windows of the bus taking us to our hotel, we were spellbound by the sight of the locals' colourful batik robes and hankies pinned onto the women's hair. With babies bound on their backs, mothers strode along gracefully, with heavy baskets and pots balanced nonchalantly on their heads.

How well I remember The Majestic, the dilapidated hotel where we spent the next two nights—where flies tasted us before they tasted our food and where, with no locks on the doors, some of us had to fight to keep our virginity. The strange animal odors in the hallways haunt me to this day.

Nothing surprised us in that hotel. One night a man's bare leg broke through the flimsy ceiling of our bedroom. I wonder if it taught him a lesson not to eavesdrop in future! On another occasion, a man dressed in white fencing gear ran through the halls flashing his sword, followed shortly by another fencer in hot pursuit. Were they ghosts or French officers fighting to the death?

During one day of our stay, a swim on the almost deserted beach was most welcome. We were beyond surprise by now, though it seemed strange to us to see lepers wandering freely around the beach. It seemed even stranger that the local whore-hut was located there, in full view of us all. It was a small circular building with swinging doors opening and closing as clients went to and fro.

We girls spent our time relaxing, sunbathing and swimming in the bright blue sea. But when we suddenly realized that the town drains emptied into that bay, we quickly dashed back to the hotel to wash before the next leg of our journey. This seemed a good idea until we had soaped all over and found there was no water left to rinse off!

✈

The nine-hour flight from Dakar to Brazil proved no smoother than the last leg as we climbed to 11,000 feet at 230 miles per hour and passed over the Doldrums to cross the equator. With bumps and jerks, the noise and vibrations threw us all over the cabin whilst we did our very best to serve our passengers. I myself felt awful. My passengers felt the same; when answering my bell I found one of them looking ashen and distraught, crying, "Please stop the plane! I'm scared and I want to get off!"

That was the most frightening crossing on our route. When the plane was full, our only hope for sleep was to lie down on the lumpy mailbags in the hold, made even more uncomfortable by the uneven movement of the plane flying through turbulence. Luckily we knew we could always rely on our courageous ex-bomber pilots, with their years of wartime experience, who got us to our destination regardless of the perils.

When we reached Natal, Brazil, we were put up in a temporary shack at the airport, having been almost asphyxiated by the awful anti-bug repellent that was sprayed all over us before we left the aircraft. During that night, the Brazilian bugs, quite oblivious of the spray, enjoyed a feast of us tasty morsels. What a price to pay to be a Star Girl!

PINEAPPLES AND SAMBA

We had just enough time to buy pineapples for the folks back home before leaving hot and humid Natal for the seven-hour journey to Rio. But a storm was gathering as we were approaching Rio, forcing our pilots to find another place to land. Low on fuel, there was nowhere else to go, so they headed for Rio again. By this time it was dark, and thunder, lightning and rain enveloped us.

The captain called us to say he could not land safely between the mountains. He would, however, try to make a box landing, which meant flying around the four sides of a square, gradually losing altitude. There we were, in complete darkness, the rain pouring down, with only the thunder to drown the sound of the droning engines.

Smoking was allowed on board in those days and by the number of cigarettes being lit, I know the passengers must have sensed trouble. However, my instructions were to just smile, sit tight and show utter calmness, which I did! When I returned to my seat to re-read my emergency and ditching drill, one of my fellow Star Girls was mortified to find that she had a ladder in her stockings. To me this seemed irrelevant, as any minute we might all be dead! In times like these, trivialities can stifle the fear that lies ahead, so I promised I'd buy her another pair in Rio.

Already we'd touched land but a second bounce would have put us in the sea, so the Captain had to hastily rev up the engines and climb again. I'm happy I'm here to recount that memorable landing, as we finally came to a stop within inches of the sea. That I was unable to put on my shoes—because my feet had swollen beyond imagination—seemed of little importance.

We were compensated that night by the luxury of our room on the 21st floor of Rio's Hotel Serrador, which promptly erased the memory of our terrifying flight. We were even able to enjoy a performance by the Brazilian samba singer Carmen Miranda in the nightclub before retiring.

Rio was magical. The next day we wandered through the shops full of colourful silks and handbags made from crocodile and snakeskin. Surely we had now found paradise, and all within earshot of the rhythmical sounds of the distant jungle.

Our next leg was from Rio to Montevideo. One advantage over the modern Boeing 747s for the passengers in the 1940s was that we had to fly so low they could actually enjoy the scenery, although Brazil offered only miles of mountain terrain covered by wild jungle growth.

One of my blunders as a Star Girl involved the Uruguayan golf team, as well as the British Ambassador, Sir Neville Butler, and his wife, who were all passengers on a flight together. Upon landing at Montevideo, the press was waiting for us on the tarmac. As I opened the aircraft door, one of the photographers jabbered at me in Spanish. Thinking he wanted to photograph the golf team, I held everyone else back whilst pushing the golf team forward. Suddenly a Star Girl who understood Spanish dashed up frantically saying, "Eve, they don't want the golf team! It's the Ambassador and his wife they're interested in." Thank goodness they all had a sense of humour. I made a mental note to continue my attempt to learn Spanish before I made any more gaffes.

Thankfully, Montevideo to Buenos Aires was a short two-hour flight. So far, on our trip, we had served 140 hot meals (not counting tea and snacks) and innumerable drinks from the bar box, and had washed thousands of pieces of china and hundreds of glasses.

Shopping in Buenos Aires was an extravaganza. While still in effect at home, rationing was not happening here, so we spent our spare pennies on meat and tinned butter, silk stockings, and leather goodies. And while we were touring the city, a handsome tango teacher fervently attempted to woo one of my colleagues, Prunella, though she rebuffed his advances. Her main worry was having the fellow see her woolly knickers!

✈

Normally, new Star Girls were not allowed to fly over the Andes to Santiago until they had been flying for at least six months. However, my captain, for some reason, did not trust leaving me on my own to entertain myself in Buenos Aires, so he took me along!

For our flight to Santiago, our aircraft was changed from a York to a Lancastrian. As that plane had not yet been properly converted for civil use, the wingspan formed a large spar between the tiny forward galley and the passenger compartment. We all knew the 18 intrepid passengers enjoyed watching us, in our tight skirts, clambering over the spar to look after their needs.

One of my passengers objected to having to do up his seatbelt. When he asked me why he must, he didn't seem to appreciate my silly answer to his silly question: "In case the tail fin falls off!"

As we were climbing to 20,000 feet over the Andes in our unpressurised cabin, we had to hastily put oxygen masks on each of the passengers before rushing to connect our own masks to the main supply. At the beginning of this leg, passengers were calm and under control, periodically looking down over their masks to the snow-covered peaks of the Andes.

But there was palpable anxiety when the captain alerted us that directly below was Mount Aconcagua, a bubbling volcano thrusting open its giant mouth to an altitude of 17,400 feet. The air temperature outside was now 25 degrees Celsius and I wished we weren't flying quite so low, as this was certainly not the best place to make an emergency landing. At that very moment, my bell rang. One of the passengers had been sick. I quickly changed over from the main oxygen supply to the portable emergency source, which allowed me only two minutes to get him organised before my own oxygen ran out.

After our white-knuckled flight, we took a well-earned weeklong break in Chile's capital, Santiago, where we and the rest of the crew enjoyed golf, tennis, mountain hiking, swimming, snorkelling and of course, chess and playing cards. Though it was March, we sunbathed on the beach while our families at home shivered in the damp cold and rain.

✈

Sadly, one of our planes, a Lancastrian named Star Dust, did not reach its destination, having mysteriously disappeared in August 1947 in the same mountains that gave us such a scare. I was scheduled to be on the Star Dust's very next flight.

In the late 1990s, wreckage from that plane was discovered by climbers in the lower reaches of a glacier in the Andes. The cause of the crash is now believed to be the jet stream that pushed the aircraft off course and into the side of a snow-packed mountain.

Two other BSAA planes had mysterious and tragic endings too. After I'd been flying for about a year in the Yorks and Lancastrians, the British Overseas Airways Corporation (BOAC) provided us with pressurised Tudor aircraft including one called Star Tiger. In January 1948, on a flight between Santa Maria Azores and Bermuda, that plane vanished from the sky. And just a year after that, another Tudor passenger plane, Star Ariel, disappeared en route from Bermuda to Jamaica, giving rise to the legend now known as the "Bermuda Triangle." After that, the Tudors were prohibited from carrying passengers, though they were used successfully as fuel carriers during the Berlin airlift.

✈

Could it really have taken a total of 20 days, including 30 hours of actual flying time, for me to go from London to Santiago? It seems a miracle that our crew survived ten of those hazardous trips! Now I fly in one of Virgin Atlantic's Airbus planes or Boeing 747s, sitting in upper class, served by an air hostess dressed immaculately in her red designer uniform. After my second glass of champagne, I sometimes meander back through the aircraft to observe more than 300 contented, relaxed passengers, marvelling at how very different it is from my flying experiences those 60 odd years ago!

CHAPTER 3

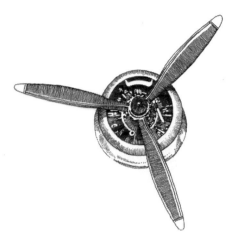

O NE NIGHT, AT A PARTY at a private home in London, my life
changed forever. The man in the corner was tall, blonde and
handsome, a young girl's dream. I looked at the plate of cocktail
sausages beside me. The way to a man's heart was surely through
his stomach, I told myself, picking up the plate. I made my way
across the room, unable to take my eyes off him. Who he was I
didn't know, but he was certainly the man I had been waiting for.
I would soon learn the name of this handsome ex-Cavalry Major:
Edward James Branson. We spent the evening reminiscing about
our wartime experiences and talking about my precarious job as
an air hostess. After all my other romances, I just knew Ted was
the man I wanted to marry, but more important, I knew he was the
man I wanted to father my future family.

✈

Ted's war experience fascinated me. In September 1939, he was
meant to go back to Trinity College, Cambridge for his third year
of reading for the Bar when war was declared. He felt that it was
more important to deal with Hitler than to qualify as a barrister, so
he volunteered and was duly commissioned into a cavalry regiment.
Everyone watched in horror as country after country fell to the

German army until almost all of Western Europe was overrun and Britain stood alone.

Despite the risk of Germany invading Britain, Churchill considered the protection of our oil supplies in the Middle East of vital importance. So a large force that included Ted sailed off in a huge convoy consisting of our biggest and fastest liners to avoid or outpace German submarines. They sailed around Africa and arrived in the Suez Canal about eight weeks later.

After a few months serving in Palestine, Ted's regiment was mechanised with tanks and then, along with the British 8th Army, faced Field Marshal Rommel's Panzer Division at the gates of Alexandria in Egypt. The ensuing battle, which lasted about 12 days and nights, resulted in Britain's first great victory over the German Army. Churchill had previously ordered that all the church bells should be silenced throughout the United Kingdom, only to be rung as a warning of an impending German invasion. In this case, though, he made an exception, ordering that they be rung in celebration of this great victory.

This first triumph was followed by a slow advance by the 8th Army through the Egyptian desert, Libya and Tunisia, some 1,100 miles. Ted next took part in two heavily covert assaults on Italy, first at Salerno, south of Naples, and then at Anzio, south of Rome, painfully and slowly driving the enemy back through the mountains.

After completing five and a half unbroken years away, he was granted leave with his family in England, during which time Germany capitulated. After his leave, he served as a staff officer in the Army of Occupation in West Germany for another year before being discharged to become a barrister. This was no ordinary man I had fallen in love with, but Ted hadn't exactly fallen for the quiet girl next door either!

After having been through the austerity of war days, you can image my surprise when I first visited Ted's home, a glorious family estate in Suffolk, Brandfield Hall, that was surrounded by acres of fields and magnificent gardens. I was quite nervous when Ted introduced me to his elderly mother and father, Sir George and Lady Mona Branson, who had six staff attending to them and their elegant home.

I'm not quite sure Sir George ever approved of his son's flibbertigibbet girlfriend, but in spite of that small point, Ted and I pressed on. His mother, on the other hand, whom I called Lady B., accepted me graciously in spite of the family's grandeur and my lack of formal social training. In turn I loved her too.

Ted also had an older sister, Joyce, who had helped to bring him up, and a half- brother named Joe Addison. Because Joe was so much older, their paths seldom crossed, though we did hear that he married a beautiful South African lass named Wendy.

Ted and I continued our blissful romance for the next few months; we spent hours at the estate playing with the dogs, riding horses and just enjoying each other's company. When he finally proposed, asking that I abandon my risky flying career for the safety of married life, I said yes! I was looking forward to another new adventure: being a wife and raising a family.

✈

Now firmly engaged, I lived in a perpetual misty dream as I planned our wedding. The fact that neither of us had a job seemed immaterial. Ted was supposed to be studying for the Bar, but mostly we spent leisurely hours roaming the fields; he carried a gun under one arm whilst I trotted behind him like a faithful spaniel.

How we enjoyed our freedom after those long war years! I remember finding bees' nests and trying to procure the honey to add to our homemade wine. We would shroud ourselves in pieces of an old veil and Ted would climb the tree and give it a good shake. I would hold the box below to catch pieces of honeycomb. The result was chaos, bees getting in every available corner but leaving their honey intact in the nest as we ran for dear life with the bees in hot pursuit!

One memorable day I took Ted to meet my Uncle Charlie, a vicar who was the curator of one of the oldest Suffolk churches. The somewhat full-figured Uncle Charlie proudly and eagerly showed us his lectern and instructed us to follow him as he climbed up a steep ladder to his belfry. All went well until, when we said goodbye, I remarked that we were thrilled to have seen his church but were also intrigued to have seen his "rectum"! On our return journey

Ted pointed out my faux pas and we had to stop the motorbike and roll around on the ground in laughter.

By now the war was fading and hunt balls were in full swing, with all the beautiful young Suffolk "punches" still lining up for this handsome bachelor, Ted. I knew I still had to be on my guard though we were already engaged, and was counting on my South American suntan to be a winning point.

One day Ted thought he'd surprise me by booking two theatre tickets. What did he choose but two front row stalls for "Bless the Bride." In no way could I confess that I had been in that show for four years, though only as an understudy. I was fearful that his father, Sir George, would not approve of having a daughter-in-law who had worked as one of Cochran's Young Ladies, who were best known for stripping on stage.

I sat silently through the first half and when I asked Ted if he was enjoying the show, he answered, "Yes, but everybody seems to be looking at me!" I worried that admitting I had been part of the show might put my engagement in the balance. Would Ted be ashamed of my past and choose a Suffolk beauty instead? Finally I decided to tell him the truth—the cast members were my friends who wanted to see who I had in tow. To my surprise, he was proud that his date was an actress!

MARRIAGE AND MOTHERHOOD

On 24 October 1949 I walked down the aisle on my father's arm in Frimley Green Church wearing my great, great grandmother's wedding dress, a white lace, off-shoulder dress that was first worn in 1843 but has a modern flair, even to this day. It was worn by three generations of brides before me and I hope it will be worn by many more to come!

Exactly where and when Richard was conceived, no one is quite sure. We spent the first night of our honeymoon at the Savoy Hotel in London, followed by a boat journey to Majorca where men and women were segregated. At last we enjoyed a wonderful stay on the island, a most romantic setting for newlyweds.

We arrived back in England with our heads in the clouds, blissfully unconcerned about where we were going to live, let alone what we were going to live on—and little did we know a baby was on the way. Ted had been receiving a small allowance from his father, who wasn't a rich man despite being a High Court judge. Ted's mother was fearful for our future and, realising we'd never made any housing arrangements, she rented a small flat for us in Camberley.

While we were settling into our flat, Ted started to study and I set about finding ways to pay the bills. Perhaps one of my crazier ideas was dashing off to Camberley to buy a job lot of pillows, then sitting in our tiny little flat taking the stuffing out of each pillow and sewing them back together, turning every one pillow into three cushions. Feathers went absolutely everywhere, but we made a bit of money— about £1 profit per cushion.

Luckily, the landlord didn't have to put up with this for long and must have been only too pleased when one day we got a letter from a dear old lady, Mrs Roma, whom I had recently befriended. She asked whether we would be interested in a condemned property she owned in Shamley Green, near Guildford in Surrey, the very village where I used to buy my sweets whilst schooling nearby at the Hallams. We went over to take a look and discovered her derelict 17th century cottage. It certainly was a wreck, with no modern conveniences, but it was full of character and overlooked the picturesque village green. With the help of Ted's parents, we were able to buy the cottage for the princely sum of £1,700—it would be our first family home.

MAKING A GO OF IT

In spring,1950, Ted was called to the Bar. It was an exciting time, living in a condemned cottage with a baby well on the way. In those days, doctors often advised pregnant women to rest as much as possible, so my mother treated me to a stay at the Maternity Nursing Home in Blackheath for the last few months of my pregnancy.

Richard, weighing 9 pounds 4 ounces, was born 18 July 1950. He was christened Richard Charles in our local church with one of my dancing friends, Sonia Flemming, as godmother and Ted's friend from the Bar, Robin Carey-Evans, as godfather, in attendance.

✈

Having started our family, money was tight but I managed to make our cottage attractive with the odd bits of leftover fabrics from my cushions. We were still getting around on our old motorbike, which was fine until Richard was two years old. I remember zipping up the hills beyond the green with Ted driving and me on the pillion, clinging to him for dear life, trying to keep my arm straight whilst pulling Richard in his pram behind. Richard thoroughly enjoyed these outings, looking around, very relaxed, although some of our stuffy neighbours didn't think our mode of transport was such a good idea.

Ted wasn't earning a fortune as a junior barrister, so I decided to double my efforts to generate income. In an attempt to utilise the few qualifications I had, I decided to teach ballet. I rented the nearby village hall at Grafham and started teaching pupils ranging in age from three to 18. But because my so-called partner, the pianist, took half the income, there was little left to pay for the time and effort I was investing.

So I continued to produce cushions and soon expanded the business to include trays and tablemats. Whilst the business was growing, so was my family, with the birth of daughter Lindy, born 30 June 1953, an 8-pound blonde and beautiful baby girl.

✈

To accommodate my expanding business, we were lent, rent-free, a little wooden shed by a dear old friend of ours, the novelist Sir Phillip Gibbs, who lived on the other side of Shamley Green. He was a super chap. Every afternoon he would play billiards with Richard and me, give us tea and send me home with a copy of The Times. We couldn't afford our own and Ted needed to read the law reports.

I was able to earn still more money, without neglecting the children, when Ted's mother treated me to a larger shed, which was grandly referred to as the "factory," situated at the bottom of our own small garden. Eventually my business grew until we had four employees. Our main sales came from Harrods, the Mayfair General Trading and other gift and fancy goods shops. My designs expanded to include boxes and tins, which I turned into objects d'art for ladies' dressing tables. When I got into making tissue boxes, the fabrication became more complicated, as each box required six separate pieces of hardboard. Ted helped by making a press that allowed us to glue the pieces together.

With my earnings from crafts and with Ted beginning to secure a few briefs, we were able to buy what we called the "bumpety-bump car," an old baker's delivery van that looked somewhat like a greenhouse on wheels. That car enabled us to go on holidays to South Devon to stay with my parents, who played a big part in our children's early lives. At times the children stayed with them for days at a time whilst we returned home so I could continue to build my business. Once a year I would pack up my wares to display at the Fancy Goods Fair in Blackpool, where I would take orders from gift shop owners from all around the country. How Ted laughed as he waved me off, seeing "Fancy Goods" emblazoned on my carriage door!

But after a few good years, my crafts business came to an abrupt halt. I was using hardboard and spray paint to create tablemats that sold very well. One day I received a letter from the office of the local fire inspector saying that they suspected I was using flammable materials in a space with insufficient ventilation. To continue working, I would have to move the business to proper factory premises. With our limited resources, this was out of the question, and I had to let my employees go. I was unhappy but not discouraged, as I knew it wouldn't be long before I could come up with another way to generate income. I always have lots of ideas!

As a young mother, I was convinced that the youth of the day were far too namby-pamby. I certainly didn't want my children to turn out that way. I was very keen that all my children should be full of initiative, enterprise, and self-reliance from an early age.

I remember overstepping the mark on one occasion. We had been on holiday in Devon and were driving back to my parents' house from Thurlstone. Richard was six at the time and was throwing himself about the car with his usual energy. I stopped the car about a mile from the house and told Richard that he should find his own way back home. Ted wondered whether it was a good idea but Richard didn't mind a challenge, so we left him to clamber over the high hedges and wander down the valley and across the fields as we drove back to the house, expecting to greet him there after a short while.

Looking back on it now, I certainly wouldn't do that again, as after an hour we began to get worried. Dusk was descending. Ted sounded the car horn every five minutes, hoping the noise would give Richard a sense of direction. By 7pm, two hours after we had dropped him off, I was beside myself, realising my mistake. I remember asking Ted, "What have I done?" I was frantic.

At 8pm, a phone call came from the only nearby farm: "We've got a little blonde boy with us who says he is Richard Branson. Does he belong to you?"

The relief was such that I swore that one day I'd help other mothers find their lost children. Perhaps that was why, years later, I ended up serving on the Board of the International Centre for Missing and Exploited Children.

Richard, quite unaware of the panic, found it great fun roaming the fields and knocking on the door of the first farmhouse he found. Was it that experience that turned him into the adventurer he is? I wonder. To be sure, this was the first of the many adventures that would famously fill his life!

✈

We always instilled in our children a sense of responsibility for those around them and encouraged them to put others' needs and comfort before their own. We taught them that the world was theirs for the taking, but it was up to them to make things happen. Being a self-starter was tremendously important. And we tried to set a good example for them in our own lives. Ted and I didn't sit them down one day and say, "Anything is possible in this world," but they understood that a lot was expected of them. Because I had always been very independent and determined myself, I looked for those traits in others.

Our philosophy was to teach our children to live every day to the fullest and not to dwell on the past. We also encouraged them not to be afraid of challenges, no matter how difficult they seemed. Richard certainly took that to heart and his seemingly endless love for dangerous exploits caused Ted and me much anxiety. To calm my nerves and distract me from thinking about the potentially disastrous outcome of his record-setting attempts, I started writing detailed accounts, moment by moment, of his adventures.

Ted and I were also of the attitude that if you were shy, you were being selfish. We would even drag the children downstairs to sing and recite in front of our dinner guests. They hated it to begin with, but soon it became second nature. After all, if you can't risk making a fool of yourself, there is little chance of achieving anything in this world. People sometimes accuse Richard of being a show-off, but it is not that at all. He is just trying to entertain others whilst forgetting himself in the process.

Sometimes it was difficult to curb Richard's exuberance and drive for fun and adventure. When visiting Clare's friend Dougy Bader, who had lost his legs in the war, Richard would sometimes hide his wooden legs, but Dougy didn't seem to mind. You'd often find him on the golf course playing with six or so children who happily had to heave him out of bunkers.

I never liked the idea of babysitters. I was sure they wouldn't have been able to cope with our very lively children, so we'd put a mattress on the backseat of our "bumpety-bump car" and take them out to dinners with us, where they'd be close at hand at all times. This was often criticized, but it seemed better at the time than trusting a stranger to look after them.

In 1956, petrol was being rationed because of the Suez Canal crisis. We were living as simply as we could; we couldn't afford extras like wine or spirits but we celebrated with Woodpecker Cider whenever Ted was paid for a brief. The empty cider bottles, with their screw tops, were ideal for one of our money-saving schemes—syphoning petrol out of our car to fill 12 cider bottles so we would always have a supply on hand. This seemed to work until the day we screwed the tops on too tightly and on contact with our kitchen gas fridge, the bottles burst and the flames not only ignited the other bottles but also the old wooden kitchen!

I ran upstairs to carry our two sleeping children down to the garden before ringing the fire brigade. Meanwhile, Ted managed to hose down the flames himself. "Don't call the fire brigade," he called out. "I've put out the fire!" We not only felt terribly guilty about

45

putting our family at risk—we also wanted to avoid embarrassing headlines in the papers.

Everyone was safe, but in carrying Richard and Lindy to safety, I ended up with three slipped discs. The result seemed disastrous to me at the time. My doctor suggested that for the rest of my life I would have to wear a steel corset. This idea was horrific, as was the thought of trying to manage our lively children when it was painful just to move.

We couldn't afford any extra help, but all worked out in the end; my next-door pal, Janie, sent in my meals each day and somehow managed to help me whilst caring for her own two children. Later my mother-in-law treated me to a bed in Guy's Hospital where, under one of the best specialists, I was ordered complete rest on a hardboard bed. The children were sent to Devon to stay with my parents, who converted their garage barn into a small flat to accommodate their young guests.

CHAPTER 4

YING ON A BOARD DAY after day in the hospital was tedious, especially on Sundays. To entertain myself, I scoured the advert columns in the newspaper. One day, a certain ad caught my eye: Menorca – Fisherman's Cottage – For Sale on Water's Edge. Sounded fun, but where was Menorca? With the help of the nurses I soon discovered it was a small Balearic Island in the Mediterranean.

A nurse brought a telephone to my bed so I could call about the cottage. A man answered the phone and said he'd come round immediately to show me a picture of the property. This certainly caused a flurry amongst the staff. "What if he's a fat, spotty con man?" "What if he's a crook?" "Surely he doesn't realise you're in hospital, flat on your back and in a corset!" The nurses exploded with laughter.

"Well, I tell you what," I said. "Put the trolley outside, cover a pillow with a sheet and if he looks like a con man, tell him I died this morning."

Moments later, in strode a tall, handsome man. Trolley, pillow and sheet were instantly removed. I was embarrassed when he saw my situation, but he didn't seem to mind. I was charmed by him and by the description of the wonderful island and property he had for sale.

I told Ted about it and, thinking it was a safe bet, he promised me if I learnt Spanish and got better, he'd consider buying me the cottage. Thank goodness he lost his bet! I did recover and started what would be a lifelong attempt to learn Spanish. Once I was on my feet again, we left the children with my parents and flew from London to Palma, Majorca, and then on to San Luis, Menorca to see the family holiday home we hoped would be as wonderful as it sounded.

✈

We soon understood why there were so few tourists on the unspoilt island of Menorca. We had to sit for seven hours at Palma Airport waiting for a connection before we joined a crowd of excited Menorcans and climbed into an old Bristol plane to fly to San Luis. We were all happily anticipating the trip: they were going to their beloved home and we had the excitement of the unknown ahead.

We arrived safely at the bumpy old airfield at San Luis after a farmer shooed his cows and sheep from the runway. Once the plane stopped, we all collected our suitcases and, as there were no Customs officers in those days, we each went on our way. Some passengers left by bicycle with their bundles strapped on; we were lucky enough to find Lorenzo, the island's only taxi driver, who took us to the Rey Carlos Hotel overlooking the beautiful Mahon Harbour.

The sales agent had described the property as a "candy house" before driving us the five kilometres to view the place, which was known as Casa Candi. It was one of only two fisherman's cottages in the charming little bay of Binibeca de Pescadore, which later became a thriving tourist destination. This idyllic cottage stood out like a sugar lump overlooking the sandy beach with two fishing boats on the slip far below. Though we were more financially comfortable than early in our marriage, we could ill afford to buy it, but buy it we were compelled to do, as it was a dream location and the price was low.

On the last day of our visit, still clad in our bathing costumes, we dashed to the notary to confirm the sale, though we knew we'd barely have time to catch our plane home. On our late arrival at the airport, we found the Bristol plane waiting for us on the tarmac, the passengers quite oblivious to our scanty attire.

✈

During our second weeklong visit, Lorenzo found us an old Barcelona taxi that had been put out to grass and was for sale for a very small sum. Having a car was essential, as there were no buses or other public transportation on the island. We also found a used boat through Lorenzo's friend, Jesus, who was the gardener for the author Harry Wilcox, one of the few English residents of the island.

I asked Jesus if he knew of any wooden Menorcan boats for sale. He was hesitant to help because boats were the fishermen's livelihood. But he took us to the sleepy little fishing village of Cala Fons to see the locals' wooden fishing boats, which are called llouts. Pointing to one named Margarita, I said, "I'd love one just like that."

Jesus disappeared into a nearby cave and promptly returned, grinning from ear to ear. "You're in luck," he said. "The fisherman died last week and that boat is for sale!" Things were looking up—first a villa, then a car and now a boat! Phew!

✈

One of the first people we met in Menorca, an English-speaking Menorcan named Nuria who owned the other fisherman's villa in Binibeca, would become our lifelong friend. It was fascinating to learn about her early life on the island, where her family owned one of the stately farms. She said they would send sacks of wheat to the San Luis baker and receive free bread for the family in return; people didn't have ovens in their houses in those days. The local Menorcan women would take their prepared lunch to the baker's oven and have a good gossip whilst it cooked.

Nuria had many talents, one of which was fishing. The three of us would go aboard Margarita near midnight as the full moon was rising, carrying a wicker flagon of wine and a bottle of the local Menorcan gin made with juniper berries. We'd then chug our way out to sea in the moonlight and throw old bread mixed with cheese into the water. The fish nearly jumped into the boat, they were so excited, and before long we'd caught a bucket load of sorrels, a Menorcan specialty.

Amazed by our haul, we took these tasty fish to a thatched beach bar run by Santiago and his family. Santiago was thrilled and bartered for them with a flagon of wine, a good exchange indeed. All were happy—he had a bucket of fish and we had our lovely wine!

Whilst fishing, Nuria told us about her town life in Mahon, which became the capital of Menorca in 1721. She told us stories about El Sereno, the town's watchman, who walked the narrow streets each night, keys to every house jangling in his pocket, knocking with his long iron hickory pole as he shouted out the hour. As he made his rounds, he would help the odd drunk by unlocking his door before seeing him safely to bed. Then he'd wend his way to snuff out yet another oil lamp. He was responsible for enforcing the nine o'clock curfew, a duty that bought him in contact with every person on his beat. Nuria said that until recently, everyone would leave their keys outside their door to show they were out

Nuria also told us the history of the Santa Maria church in the centre of the square. She said there were many shipwrecks off the coast of Mahon in the 18th and 19th centuries. One ship included among its cargo a large organ, brought by the British during the 18th century. It had 3,120 pipes, 250 of them wooden. The storm was such that the captain shouted over the raging winds, "If we ever get to shore alive, wherever that might be, that's where we'll leave this damn organ!" The shore where they landed was Menorca and the organ found a home in the Gothic parish church of Santa Maria.

Nuria said when she was growing up, Mahon had few modern amenities. Water was precious; until 1968, it was carried in barrels on the backs of donkeys and brought into the town from country wells. The houses were painted in white caul made of lime and water; precious rainwater was caught on their roofs in cisterns called aljibes.

When cars started appearing on the island, Nuria remembered seeing a woman driving an old yellow Citroen down the steep hill above Mahon Harbour. The brakes didn't work and she drove right into the harbour! After she swam ashore, an obliging diver went down and with the help of a crane, lifted her car out. "That's not my car," she cried. "My car is yellow!"

For those without a car, the Ferry Port taxi man would charge them the equivalent of a penny to row across the harbour or two pennies to row around the harbour to the stores.

✈

Every summer we took part in the blessing of the boat procession, known as "La Fiesta de Carmen," that happened on the 15th of July. To celebrate their Christian faith, people took to the sea in boats whilst flags waved from the naval base, fires blazed from the land and people on board the many different vessels sang "Ave Maria" and religious naval songs, accompanied by guitars.

We certainly had fun in those days. I remember when there were only four ex-patriot-owned British boats berthed by the Yacht Club. The elegant steps called "pigtail steps" led up to the American bar in the square where we would gather each morning for a snifter and a leisurely chat.

One day we arranged a car rally with 20 cars that had been all spruced and polished in the local garages. Among them were an Alfa Romeo, a Fiat 124 Coupé, a Triumph, Stag, a Ferrari Spider, a Lancia, an old Rolls, a Maserati and a 1925 Erskine.

We all dressed to suit the period and set off for lunch in the harbour of Fornells. The old Rolls I was riding in had a dickey with a large wicker basket full of champagne and water. At each hill we'd have to stop and fill up our glasses, ever hopeful we'd make it to the top. Once we'd arrived, another snifter was needed to give thanks that we'd made it.

✈

We also enjoyed shopping in Menorca, especially San Luis. The shopkeepers considered their career a noble one and indeed it was: they served their customers with grace and dignity. To fill our hand-woven eight-gallon glass casket with wine and Menorcan gin (a legacy of the British occupation in the 18th century), we'd go down to the depth of Juan's cellar where we'd spend happy hours tasting his latest wines and learning about Menorcan folklore. Then we'd go out into the sunshine to shop, perhaps to buy a pair of Abarca, Menorcan sandals made from used rubber tires, which were guaranteed to last a lifetime!

There was little variety of processed food on the island in the early days, but we enjoyed what they offered—bacon, tea, gentleman's relish and mayonnaise, which was a recipe created by

Nelson's chef at the time of British rule (hence the name Mahon-naise).

We especially loved the old Mahon market. We'd sling our baskets over our shoulders and buy carrots, huge gnarled tomatoes, scrawny chickens and ensaimadas, a large flat pastry sold in octagonal boxes. Above the market was the empty prison; when we asked shopkeepers why it was empty, they said there was no need to keep anyone prisoner and besides, they'd lost the key!

During the afternoon, we'd put a ladder on Margarita and chug around to Cala Coves, where we'd climb up into the caves that had been inhabited thousands of years before by early cave dwellers known as troglodytes. Since then, many different civilisations including Phoenicians, Greeks and Carthaginians had populated the island. Ted was in his element there, finding bones and Bronze Age needles and coins. What a shame he didn't become an archaeologist instead of a barrister.

In the evenings we'd often go to Cala Fons, a tranquil cave below the steep, cobbled hill, where a few fishing boats were moored outside the Cavé Bar. Here the locals would gather for a late night snifter of sherry or Pomada cocktail of Menorcan gin and fresh lemon juice. They'd sing and drink whilst the guitarists played, with everyone joining the chorus under a moon that flickered on the tranquil emerald green waters beyond.

The other evening entertainment we loved was the old theatre at Villa Carlos known as El Salon. In days past, because there were so few women on the island, sailors would dress up burlesque-style in black tights and costumes. They continued this tradition for years, because both locals and tourists loved it.

During the day, we spent many happy hours touring the countryside with its bright green Mediterranean pines, brown and red farmlands, pastures dotted with rocks and framed by dry stone walls, and rich vegetation opening out onto white sandy beaches.

I've always loved Menorca's climate and terrain. Both in the chilly winter and very hot summer, we'd find crashing seas and a rugged countryside where the Tramontana winds lashed out in unexpected fury. In the North, undulating hills reach no higher than the monastery on Mount Toro, 358 metres high, with a solitary lighthouse standing guard on the cliff below.

One day we managed to drive our old taxi up to the monastery where the monks rewarded pilgrims for making the trip by giving them a glass of wine. When we arrived, a bearded monk opened a little trap door, shoved two glasses of wine through it, and promptly closed the hatch!

Driving back to Mahon, we passed grand farmsteads with small red tomato clusters hanging on every spare wall and large yellow pumpkins and melons balanced on stone walls nearby. Tucked away within these gracious farms were the Arabian horses that appeared every year in one of the eight municipal area festivals that commemorated each area's own saint's day.

At the annual Fiesta of Saint Joan, which began in Menorca before the Middle Ages, the local priest, accompanied by a local band, plays on his panpipe as he leads on his donkey, followed by 20 or so horses and riders (known as caixers) dressed in medieval garb. The horses enter the square amidst great shouting and clapping, with the horsemen representing the Christian farmers and the youth on foot representing the Arab invaders.

Finally the horses—seeming to love every minute of the splendour—rise up on their hind legs and walk, almost dancing to the rhythmic beat and clapping of the crowd. Then the young boys run forward and try to bring the horses down to their feet without touching them.

✈

Our family found a second home in Menorca. Our house, Humble Pie, was the site of countless family gatherings and celebrations. We were happy when Richard later purchased property there too. We loved the beauty of the place and appreciated the individualism and pride of the islanders. Indeed, their philosophy is beautifully captured in these words, once spoken by a Menorcan bishop:

We ask you to respect us for what we are. We have a rich history and deep-rooted customs, a language that we love and a culture that gives us our identity. If we respect each other, love each other mutually, and maintain an open attitude and dialogue, all our lives will be enriched.

CHAPTER 5

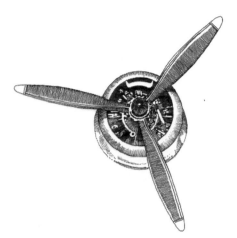

WHILE IN MENORCA, I HIT upon the idea of setting up a new business to replace my crafts endeavor: letting and selling Menorcan properties to English clients with the help of Nuria, who would find properties that I would photograph and market in England. After we'd made a few sales, I took on a secretary and opened up a property company in London called Binibella. (Many names in Menorca start with "Bini," which is Arabic for "son of" or "land of" and I liked the sound of "bella.")

The office was in a small attic at No. 13 New Bond Street. I took on a young man, a Menorcan property agent, and before long Binibella became quite successful at letting and selling island properties. As time went on, the business was a good excuse to visit Menorca, leap over the rocks, photograph the properties and bring back the details to advertise in The Times. What I didn't realise then was that my "property agent" was a crook, a scam artist who had invented his credentials.

One day, out of the blue, I received a letter saying that my company was being sued. Apparently, some of our clients' deposits had been disappearing into the man's Swiss bank account. Thinking back, I recall that he had started to behave somewhat strangely and I had half-suspected something was amiss. Every time I went to Menorca to collect my commission, he managed to hasten back to England. He was eventually caught but we lost all our commissions—about £6,000.

I was learning the hard way. After a court case in Cambridge in which I had to prove that he and I were associates and not partners, he ended up in prison and I, somewhat poorer but wiser!

By this time Binibeca was becoming popular and overcrowded, so I decided to exchange Casa Candi for Venezia, the very best house on my books. This unique house stood in the middle of the harbour, alone on a rock, connected to land by a long causeway, with a dock for a boat beneath the house. After we bought the place, we installed a glass floor above the boat dock. I had hoped to keep Venezia in the family, but the ownership of this Menorcan gem eventually reverted back to the state.

✈

On one visit to Menorca, Ted couldn't come due to his work, but a friend asked me if I'd like to take along her beautiful 21-year-old daughter, Sally, to help me. With only my secondhand taxi for transport and a remote house, this seemed like a good idea. I was somewhat hesitant, though, as I was aware that the girl had been recently diagnosed as a manic depressive. Her mother assured me that provided Sally took her medication, she'd be fine.

She was fine only until the end of our first day, when she suggested we go to the Cavé Bar in Cala Fons, which she'd heard was very lively. As she had spent the day dutifully sewing curtains, I agreed and, making sure Sally had taken her pills, drove the five kilometres to Mahon in our old taxi.

The Cavé Bar was indeed lively, with the locals drinking and singing while the guitars did their best to follow. Against the backdrop of a full moon twinkling in the peaceful harbour and fishing boats securely tied to their buoys, the bar filled with revelers and the festivities heated up.

Midnight came, the music ended, and everyone left to go home—with no one remaining but me and the barman, Santiago. Where was Sally? And where was the bar owner? Santiago was eager to close the Cavé shutters and go home, but I was starting to panic. "I can't leave without my friend. Where could she be?" I begged Santiago for help, though he barely understood a word of English.

Shrugging his shoulders, he pulled down the shutters and turned the key. Seeing my desperation, he offered to come home with me. "But, but…" I stammered, aware of the compromising position I was getting into. But what else was I to do? The idea of driving alone in that old banger along a deserted road, barely knowing the way, was not a thought I relished. But Sally was nowhere in sight and Santiago and I could only assume she'd slipped away with the owner of the Cavé Bar.

Driving Santiago home the next morning was somewhat embarrassing. Every time we passed through a village, he would duck down in the car, lest any of his friends found out that he'd spent the night with an unknown English lass!

It turns out that Sally, who until that night had been a virgin, had indeed fallen head over heels in love with the bar owner, Carlos, who was married. Though Sally had different ideas, in no way was he interested in more than a one-night stand, so the next day he dropped her back at home, to my great relief. I will never forget that night. Santiago was also a working policeman, and we never passed each other on the street after that without a wink and a smile!

The drama continued in the days ahead, as Sally was on a high with boundless energy. On several occasions I had to hide the car keys, fearful she would get in trouble with the car whilst driving. I opposed her will at my peril; once she tried to set fire to my villa before running off in the rain barefoot to find her new lover. The only safe place I could find for her was under the dryer at the only hairdresser's on the island, where, with the hood down, I knew she was secure for at least an hour and I could relax. There she would sit and scribble crazy notes about her impending marriage to Carlos.

With only one telephone on Menorca, I felt terribly isolated and was anxious to get her home. She had other ideas, of course, having no intention of leaving Carlos or the island. We missed plane after plane when she locked herself in the airport loo. Finally I had to phone her parents to come and help. When they finally arrived, accompanied by two doctors, they sedated the poor girl and managed to get her home for treatment.

This story has a happy ending. Some 30 years later I saw Sally again. She told me the medication she was taking in Menorca had been the cause of her erratic moods! She remembered everything vividly, so with apologies for all the trouble she'd caused for me and the islanders, we embraced, thankful to meet again, with our memorable adventures behind us.

✈

When Vanessa Gay was born in 1959, Ted and I felt that our family was complete. She was an adorable child, curious and energetic, who was a constant source of joy to us. So I already had my hands full when I was elected to become Justice of the Peace in Guildford. In those days you were chosen by recommendation from a judge or member of the Bar, after which you had to pass the test of having tea with the chairman of the Bench's wife to see if she thought you were suitable. I must have eaten my cucumber sandwich and sipped my tea in the appropriate fashion, for the next thing I knew, I had been sworn in.

After various courses, I was finally sitting alongside the chairman of the Bench in the Guildford Court as a "winger," trying county cases ranging from motoring offences to murder. There I was—a dancer, a signaller, an air hostess and sometime real estate agent with not much education. Perhaps it was one's life experience that was the essential ingredient to becoming a good JP!

Around the same time, a friend and I dipped a toe in publishing, having started a magazine for the blind called *The Talking Newspaper*, which entailed providing a cassette recorder for every registered blind person in our area. Each week I gathered the local news and, with other volunteers, recorded the news on cassette tapes and delivered them to the blind. After a few days, we'd pick them up to record the next week's news. Our readers soon multiplied and I'm proud to say *The Talking Newspaper* still enjoys a large readership.

FROM SCHOOLBOY TO STUDENT

Richard, now 8, had reached the age where we needed to make a decision about his education. It seemed right that he should now board, as his exuberance was rather like that of a fiery stallion. We were fearful lest we pull the reins too hard either way, yet cautious not to dampen his enthusiasm. None of the local schools were quite suitable for him; he needed more of a challenge.

CHAPTER 5

I had to be in court a day or two a week, and was busy with my various business schemes, as my small home industry was going strong. Orders still came from all the big department stores and I had to personally deliver each order by driving 20 miles to London in the old "bumpety-bump car." Ted was also busy at the bar, so neither of us felt we could give Richard the attention he needed. Ted was against sending him away, as he hadn't had a very happy time himself at boarding school, but eventually we both agreed it was a good idea. So Richard started at Scaitcliffe Preparatory School, a family-run boarding school just outside of Windsor. In spite of feeling homesick at first, he settled in and ended up thoroughly enjoying himself.

He excelled at games, captaining the football, cricket and rugby teams, and I was proud every year at Prize Giving, when mothers were called upon to collect their sons' prizes. But we were concerned about his academic progress. Yes, he was popular, but as time passed, he had become quite unruly and cared not one iota about his own education. We were soon to discover the drastic consequences of that attitude.

One day we had an emergency phone call from Richard's school matron at Scaitcliffe saying he had torn a ligament behind his knee playing in a football match. Whilst he was incapacitated, we became very worried. He was marvellous at sport but we were worried about his prospect for success on the Common Entrance exam, which by then was just a year away. We decided the only thing to do was send him away to a crammer.

We chose Cliff View House, a crammer in Seaford, Sussex, where it was all work and no games. Richard had no option but to concentrate on the Common Entrance—or so we thought. We later found out that he had almost been expelled for climbing through the window of the headmaster's daughter's bedroom late one night. I gather Charlotte, an attractive 18-year-old, had taken quite a fancy to him. Richard was tall for his age and very good-looking, with blue eyes and blonde hair.

That night ended when, upon hearing a pursuer's footsteps, he slid down the drainpipe and ran across the playing fields, knowing he had been found out! Somehow he managed to get away with the night's escapade and his expulsion was overturned.

Much to our relief, Richard pulled off another feat a year later when he not only passed his Common Entrance but sailed through with high marks. We were very keen for him to go to a good public school and thought that Stowe was the best place for this rather unusual son of ours.

We always knew he had great potential yet we weren't at all sure what to make of him. Ninety percent of the time he was impossible to discipline. As for the other ten percent, something very special was going on. Unfortunately, no one could pin down exactly what it was and there was no one to turn to for advice.

A poem he wrote at age 13 seemed to reveal his own internal struggles:

Ambition
Walking along corridors
With a block of concrete hovering over my head
Made of ambition and responsibility.
It becomes larger and larger every day,
And more and more sinister.
Will it become gold?
Or will it collapse and shatter upon me?
Or will it rapidly diminish into the distance?

✈

Lindy and Vanessa were easy to raise. We gave Lindy one of the cowsheds, which she turned into a painting studio, covering the walls with beautiful murals. Vanessa was keener on riding her pony and loved riding into the woods to have a picnic with her best girlfriend.

But raising Richard was different. He would never sit and read a book or do things quietly. He was always out and about, charging around on his bicycle or climbing trees. I remember on one occasion he went off with Nik Powell, a local friend of his, who later became a partner at Virgin before setting up Palace Pictures. Nik's parents had just given him a new bike, which the boys dared each other to ride down a hill to the river. Rather like James Dean, the idea was to jump off the bike at the last moment. On his turn, Nik leapt clear at the water's edge. Richard, of course, didn't jump off at all and went headlong into the river. He was all right but Nik's new bike was ruined. Ted and I felt we had to stump up the money for a replacement. Our adventurous son could be rather costly!

Nonetheless, I was terrified of being too stern with him because I didn't know what damage I might do. If he were naughty, I would tell him to put out his hand. I would never actually smack him; the threat was enough, although no doubt he was feigning fear as much as I was pretending to punish him. I would also warn him that his father would have strong words with him when he got home, but he never did. Ted would arrive home exhausted, still needing to read his briefs for the next day. So Richard would be off the hook yet again!

✈

The Easted cottage was beginning to feel too small for our growing family. One lucky day I saw a "For Sale" notice outside Tanyards, an empty 16th century manor farmhouse on the other side of Shamley Green. Peering through cobwebbed windows, I saw an old pot of Evo-Stik glue. That was it! I would buy the old mansion—it had literally called my name!

Our old cottage had appreciated in value and we were able to sell it for quite a sum; having bought it for £1,700, we were pleased to sell it for £17,000. Ted had switched to a criminal practice from common law so we were able to buy Tanyards right away. The children were wild about the place, with so much room to roam. The property consisted of about four acres, the farmhouse, a hand-dug pool surrounded by old barns, and a derelict cottage, which we eventually made habitable in order to let for students. We gave Lindy one of the stables to convert into a bedroom and a studio space where she could experiment with her artwork.

The old farmhouse seemed to inspire the entrepreneur in Richard. One Easter holiday when he was home from Stowe, he bought 800 little Christmas trees for £5 and planted them at the top of the garden. In four years he reckoned he would be £800 the richer, as Christmas trees were selling £1 a foot. He lost interest in the project when rabbits began to feast on the baby shoots, but we thought it had been a healthy sign of initiative.

He was more ambitious with his next project, as he was convinced his fortune lay in budgerigars because they bred quickly. They did indeed; the first pair he bought rapidly turned into 20. All of Ted's free time was spent making cages and a large aviary that soon dominated the barns, while Richard was losing interest more quickly than the birds could breed. Twenty budgies turned into 100, and it was left to me to feed and water them.

What with my own work, I had neither the time nor the love required to care for his budgies. One morning, I am ashamed to say, I left the aviary door wide open and watched them fly away to their freedom. They were happy and so were we. Richard didn't mind, as he was already planning his next money-making scheme!

✈

Things were going from bad to worse with Richard's academic standing at Stowe. He just wouldn't settle down to his school work, despite our constant harping on about the need for qualifications. Imagine our consternation when one day he rang up to say he wanted to leave. He was barely 15. He then told us about *Student*, a magazine he was proposing to launch in which he would interview famous people who were willing to share their knowledge with students. He and his friend were working on this project, mostly under the covers at night in their dormitory. The headmaster had tried to get him to work on *Stoic*, the school magazine, to no avail. Richard had his own idea and he was adamant about his magazine being a nationwide publication.

We tried to explain to Richard that he couldn't leave unless he had passed at least one A level exam. For weeks after that we didn't hear much from him. The next thing we heard was that he had passed his A level in ancient history after only one year in the sixth form. I remember him saying, "Can I leave now? You told me to get an A level and I've got one." Reluctantly we kept to our word!

By now we were both extremely concerned about his future. We had long hoped he would get the qualifications to go to Cambridge and follow in his grandfather and father's footsteps, but it wasn't to be.

✈

CHAPTER 5

After Richard left Stowe, just before he turned 17, he went straight to London with his friend, Jonathan Holland Gems, to launch *Student* magazine. They both worked madly, like men possessed, in a dark, dank, sparsely furnished church crypt lent to them by a kind vicar. Working from outdated "Who's Who" listings, they wrote to everyone, inviting contributions and subscriptions to the magazine. Sometimes they got letters back saying, "Sorry, Mr Jenkins Powell is no longer with us. He died 10 years ago." Sometimes they were lucky to find some famous old boy still alive who gave them an amazing article for no fee.

Nevertheless we were terribly worried. I brought a big basket of food every time I visited; I felt like the Red Cross parachuting in emergency supplies. I would find the boys sitting on the floor in the crypt surrounded by old coffins for furniture. They were completely absorbed in their magazine and quite disinterested in their surroundings.

The vicar must have been fascinated by what they were doing, as he invited Richard, at age 18, to give a sermon in his church! This proved a popular choice with a full congregation, though you can imagine in the 1960s that his sermon was unlike any other preached from the same pulpit. I'm only sad that it wasn't recorded.

Living in the rent-free crypt, he and Jonny were able to print the first copy of *Student* magazine in 1968. Expecting an income, they also opened a bank account. Richard chose our family bank, Coutts & Co in the Strand, which readily accepted him, but shortly after they might have regretted it. To help sell the magazine, Jonny and Richard recruited unemployed youths who would sell the magazine on the streets of London and deposit their earnings into the Coutts account. Imagine the bank employees in their smart dress suits receiving these shoeless, long-haired youths who emptied their pockets into Richard's bank account!

In the seven editions of *Student*, Richard and Jonny managed to print interesting interviews with Vanessa Redgrave, Dudley Moore, David Hockney, Mick Jagger and others. Feature articles such as "Easy Sex—Not So Easy Sex," "White Slavery Today" and "The Educational Scheme" were par for the course. However, some of the glossy covers were somewhat explicit for the time. One was of a beautiful young girl, naked and pregnant, kneeling sideways, artistic by today's standards but somewhat shocking in those days.

The less Ted and I knew about Richard's life in the next few years, the better. He was getting in with a certain crowd and standing on soapboxes at Hyde Park corner—God knows what he was saying! We felt teenagers should always be free to work their own way through those tricky years; if we hadn't instilled in him the true values of life at an early age, it was certainly too late now. Anyhow, we had our own lives to lead and two young daughters to worry about. All we asked was for him to consider us his friends and confidants and to come to us for advice should he need it.

When he did come home to visit, he was a wonderful brother to his sisters. Lindy was at Art College and, despite our best efforts, was going through a shy phase. Richard would write all her love letters. He adored writing, and they were romantic, believable letters!

At the time, I seldom ventured up to London, although I had always wanted a small pied-à-terre for the family there. So when the opportunity arose, I acquired a short lease on a rather nice house in Albion Street, a fashionable area near Marble Arch. The house was owned by the Church Commissioners and because the lease stipulated that no business was to be conducted from the property, we leased it in my name. We told Richard he could have a small room and we would live in the rest of the house.

The house was unfurnished, so I spent my time happily shopping at jumble sales and markets, buying furnishings and turning it into quite a smart property. What I didn't realise was that Richard had other ideas for the place. Using the slogan "Our Headache and Your Headaches," he had started an advisory council through *Student* that offered help to any youngster in trouble on help-phone lines. Some needed advice with unwanted pregnancies; others were in need of emotional support. Being generous, Richard would often offer them a bed in 44 Albion Street, which filled up rather quickly!

Some of the help lines received calls from youth who thought they may have venereal diseases. But before long, because the law at the time forbade publicly offering assistance to people confirmed to have such a disease, charges were brought against Richard. Barrister John Mortimer, acting pro bono on Richard's behalf, argued in court against the outdated law, calling for the law to be changed so the word "venereal" could be used without recrimination.

CHAPTER 5

In the end, with the support of the press behind him, Richard was fined only seven pounds for the offence. It was typical of Richard to want to help others, regardless of the consequences. By now we knew that it was no longer worth trying to talk him into getting a proper job. But we were also quite worried about what was going on at 44 Albion Street.

✈

Down at Shamley Green, I had become involved with a far less glamorous publication—the local church magazine. I was walking up a remote lane one day, delivering copies, when I saw something glistening on the road. It was a pearl necklace. I looked around. There was no one about, so I took it to the police station.

"Madam," the policeman said, "you do realise that if this is not claimed within three months, it is yours."

Imagine my joy when, three months later, the same policeman rang to say the necklace was unclaimed. I took it to London and went from jeweller to jeweller and was eventually offered £100, which was quite a lot of money in those days.

Hastening back to Albion Street, I handed over the bounty to Richard, the neediest person I could think of. Richard and Jonny barely had time to look up and say thanks, so immersed were they in their work. To this day, though, I like to think that the person who lost her necklace in Shamley Green played a small part in launching the Virgin Empire.

By now Ted and I realized that my dream London house was rapidly changing from what I'd intended it to be. Whilst Richard was taking down-and-outs off the streets and giving them a home, everything I bought for the house got broken or simply disappeared.

The Church Commissioners had heard that something was amiss there and we received a stern letter making it clear that the premises were not to be used for business purposes. One day, one of them rang up Richard to say he would be coming down to inspect the property.

Richard was on the phone to me within minutes, asking me to bring every toy I could find. Vanessa and I quickly gathered all the dolls, teddy bears and dinky toys in our house and brought them to London. Richard set about turning the place into a family home, just like that! He found some furniture, told all of his wayward guests to hide in the cupboards or in the basement, and then greeted the Commissioner with a broad grin, with Vanessa and me standing quietly by. The commissioner thought the place was fine, although he did look somewhat surprised when the telephone rang from a closed cupboard. If only he knew—or did he?

✈

As time passed, we fixed up the old cottage on the Tanyards property to generate income by letting it to young law students studying in Guildford. This certainly bought life to the place, although their Friday night drinking bouts worried me, especially when they invited Ted to join them! They had all been cricket players at Cambridge, so I would drag them out of bed every Saturday to coach the local village boys in our garden. The local boys soon formed a team, calling themselves the "Colts."

Realising the boys had little money to buy their pads, bats and whites, we gave a dance in the barn at Tanyards to raise money for them. After an infuriating article in the local rag claiming Shamley Green had nothing to offer but bricks and mortar, my Colts proved themselves. Dressed immaculately in white, they were finally allowed to play on Shamley Green. With a name I gave them—the "Bricks and Mortar Colts Team"—they won most of their matches. I'm especially proud to report that some of these boys went on to play cricket professionally.

BAIL, "BELLS," AND A VIRGIN ISLAND

In 1971, Richard was selling pop records through his Virgin Mail Order, a seemingly harmless enterprise that was very nearly his undoing. I was in Menorca when I received an urgent telephone call from him. When he heard my voice he broke down, explaining that he had been arrested and wanted me to come home immediately. It was a devastating blow to me, as he was only 21. I felt sick—angry, fearful, sympathetic, confused. I told him he'd have to be a man, face up to his wrongdoings, and pull himself together whilst I got on the next plane to London. It was a costly trip, but money didn't matter, given the prospect ahead. I knew I needed to keep calm and show Richard my own strength and dignity in the face of this impossible situation.

On my return to England, I discovered that Richard had devised a clever, entirely illegal scheme to avoid purchase tax on records, which was all too complicated for me to understand. He did this a few times until Customs caught up with him, whereupon he was taken to Dover Police Station, charged under the Customs and Excise Act of 1952 and spent the night in custody.

The next morning I took the train to Dover to attend the hearing. Richard was quite clearly mortified at what he had done. I was mortified too, as both Ted and I held positions in the legal system! When Richard found himself in trouble, he would normally turn to me rather than Ted because he was too ashamed to talk to his father. I felt he was often trying to prove something to Ted, knowing that Ted found it hard to be proud of his son's somewhat unusual career. When it went wrong, of course, it was doubly galling.

With no money for the £30,000 bail and with little money saved, the only thing left to do was put our house—our only asset—up as surety. I'll always remember looking across the court at Richard and for the first time in my life wondering if I could trust him. Our eyes met. He knew what I was thinking: we had given him a free rein and let him get on with his life—and here we were putting everything we'd worked for on the line for him. He was testing our relationship to the breaking point. It was an important moment.

He was granted bail and released and we caught the train back to London together, sitting in absolute silence. I could almost hear his mind racing. Crime was out of character for Richard. What he had done was more of a huge risk he'd decided to take that could have potentially grievous consequences. After what we had just been through, I felt confident that he was never going to break the law again. It was the best early lesson he could ever have learnt.

After lengthy correspondence between Ted and Customs, they agreed to drop the charge if Richard paid £15,000 immediately and a further £45,000 fine over the next three years. With help from his Aunt Joyce, Ted's sister, and great determination on his part, he managed to pay the fines and thus avoid a criminal record.

✈

But happier days were ahead for Richard: soon he would meet Kristen, a beautiful, tall, blonde American. She totally captivated not only Richard but the family too. Ted and I were happy that he seemed to be moving toward a more normal life, with a personal relationship to balance out his interest in business.

As he was getting more and more involved in the music business, he bought a wonderfully grand manor house outside Oxford. Coutts & Co was only too ready to lend money in those days, and Joyce agreed to stand as a guarantor. Richard converted the manor's squash court into a recording studio and once again I helped him furnish the place. I remember finding an antique grandfather clock on sale, although a bed or two might have been money better spent!

One weekend we were summoned there to hear some music that Richard and his cousin, Simon Draper, were absolutely mad about. They got a big roaring fire going in the sitting room where there was one old sofa for guests.

"Just shut your eyes and listen, Mum and Dad." Then he put on this dreadful music at full volume and all we could think was that it was the most dissonant sound we'd ever heard. We were speechless. It turned out to be music from Mike Oldfield's "Tubular Bells." Mike was there, so thank goodness we didn't make our views known. Of course, the record went on to make Richard and Simon a small fortune and is still considered a bit of a masterpiece today. They never looked back and we later came to love the sound of "Tubular Bells"!

✈

Although Kristen was just 20 and Richard only 22, they decided to get married and chose the manor as the site for their wedding, an event which would be half conventional and half contemporary. Richard's staff hired top hats from Moss Bros for the men in the wedding party. Long hair for men was the fashion in 1972, and we found it somewhat charming and most amusing to see top hats perched on young men with hair straggling down their shoulders!

Invitations were sent to all the local villages, the Virgin staff, several rock bands and both families. On the day of the wedding, all was going according to plan except that my 74-year-old mother had not arrived. Just before the service was scheduled to start, a large articulated lorry arrived and a little old lady alighted, dressed in her wedding finery—it was Mummy! After apologising for being late, she explained that her car had broken down and she'd hitched a lift, for there was no way she was going to miss her grandson's wedding!

✈

Soon Richard was working from his Thames houseboat Duende, which was situated on the canal opposite Blomfield Road in Little Venice; this became both his home and headquarters in London. All work and meetings took place on the glass rooftop Richard had constructed there. One's mind boggled at what various luminaries thought as they arrived at a little wooden gate and walked the narrow path to the "office" on the boat.

His business was going so well that in February of that year, he gave Ted and me two weeks' notice for a fortnight's holiday anywhere we wanted, to be executed quickly or he might change his mind. Thrilled, we settled down on a rainy winter's evening devouring atlases, encyclopaedias, brochures and a stack of glossy travel magazines.

Our final choice was the luxury Cariblue Hotel on the island of St. Lucia. We made a quick dash to buy shorts and sandals; I was happy to replace my frumpy JP's wardrobe with colourful clothes suitable for a Caribbean adventure.

Vanessa planned to join us after a few days. When she arrived, however, she found that the hotel had been overbooked and she had the choice of sleeping on the beach or in our room with us. The hotel staff set up an extra bed in our suite and we three made the best of the situation.

While the powers-that-be were sorting out our rooming problems, we wasted no time starting our holiday. Ted and Vanessa secured two sprightly horses and galloped out to Pigeon Island whilst I played golf with Meiling, a German lady I'd just met who was looking for a golfing partner.

That night Meiling asked if we'd seen the notice saying that because the hotel was overbooked, they were offering a free week aboard a yacht, with a skipper and cook on board, that would visit most of the Grenadine Islands. Meiling and the three of us put our names down, and almost instantly we had a yacht to ourselves! It was like a dream come true.

En route to the beautiful Tobago Quays, we toured Bequia, Petit Nevis and Mustique. About 15 islands were situated close together, all with golden sandy beaches and palm trees. Yachts were moored near each island in water that was every shade of blue and green, with a scattering of silver bubbles emerging like shooting stars from below. At one point Vanessa shouted, pointing upwards. She had seen a large blue and white spinnaker from a nearby yacht floating up into the sky with a man attached. Panic! Ted and I got into our dinghy to offer our help. As we approached, we heard shouting and laughter and discovered they were performing the art of spinnaker flying. Silly me—I had never seen the sport before.

On the seventh day of the trip we reached Palm Island. The beauty was so breathtaking that we didn't know whether we should thank the Lord that we were alive to witness such beauty or thank him for the son who had enabled us to experience such a place. Little did we know that Richard was also exploring the Caribbean with his own thoughts of purchasing a private island.

Finally we caught a small plane back to St. Lucia where the manager and directors of the Cariblue were anxious to hear how we fared. We told them it had been divine. As far as I was concerned, if this was the result in overbooking, I only hoped they were overbooked again if we were ever fortunate enough to return!

✈

Our family continued to grow and thrive. In 1976, Lindy married Robert Abel Smith in a ceremony at Tanyards, where I had decorated the barns with autumn flowers. We would soon say goodbye to Vanessa too, as we decided that she would benefit from being at a co-educational school. So we sent her to Boxhill and then to courses in secretarial skills, Spanish, cooking and interior design. She later studied the history of art.

Lindy was an extraordinarily talented artist who would go on to become a superb painter and sculptor. Vanessa would also become involved in the arts—like her brother, she had an affinity for starting businesses. Having been an apprentice picture framer with Richard Fitzgerald in Soho, she opened her own firm, Poster Brokers, in

Fulham, where she offered framing services and represented artists as well.

With the girls gone from home and Richard still making his way in London, I found myself needing some excitement. Luckily I didn't have long to wait, as one morning Ted and I were stunned to receive a call from the Governor of Tortola, the capital of the British Virgin Islands, asking us to send him Richard's dossier. Just what was he up to now? An immediate call to Richard's secretary, Penni Pike, put us in the picture. Richard was trying to buy Necker, one of the last uninhabited Virgin Islands in the Caribbean. The Governor would not give his permission until he was thoroughly satisfied that Richard was an honest English citizen, so we were asked to give our son a reference, an assignment we thoroughly enjoyed!

The Governor also checked with Who's Who, CBS, EMI Records and even Warner Brothers. Still not content, he checked with Coutts & Co, Richard's London bank, to find out if he was indeed honourable. Lo and behold, he was!

EXPLORING AN UNINHABITED ISLAND

A few months later we got a last-minute invitation from Richard to inspect his new acquisition, an island inhabited by a few families of goats. He had already been to the island with Joan Templeman, a stunning young Scottish woman he'd met a few years before, after he and Kristen had decided to part ways. He and Joan loved the island, though it was truly uncharted, virgin territory. Could we be ready to leave in a week's time? Of course we would! Richard gave us strict instructions to take not only the usual bikinis and swimming costumes but also golf shoes and long trousers, the importance of which we would soon discover.

Excited, we arrived at Heathrow's Terminal 3 on a cold spring day. The eight-hour flight to Antigua seemed like a short bus ride as we were both engrossed in the literature provided by the Caribbean Sailing Yachts Association (CSY). We were still studying when we touched down smoothly at Antigua Airport.

Our 90-minute hop to Tortola in a 24-seat plane was fun and the scenery was gorgeous as we approached the Virgin Islands. Flying low over the ocean ranging in color from turquoise to jade to indigo, we lost count of the many small islands and the bright white sails of hundreds of boats.

At Tortola Airport, we were greeted by our American friends, Kristen's parents Joe and Jackie, and we all set off in a taxi, twisting and turning along the coastline until we reached our hotel, the Prospect Reef.

What joy, having left the smog of London, to find that the temperature was 80 degrees! We settled in at the bar by the Yacht Basin, all four of us sipping our drinks and enjoying the view when, suddenly, right in front of us, six pelicans in perfect formation dive-bombed simultaneously, emerging a few seconds later with their bills filled with fish. It took them a minute or two to syphon out the water and give a satisfied swallow before taking off once more, still in formation, to circle the hotel before repeating the procedure. Surely even the Red Arrows could have learnt something from this performance.

We would spend the next few days sailing to Peter Island, Marina Cays, Virgin Gorda and Prickly Pear Island before meeting up with Richard at Necker. Before Richard and Joan, only two other people had ever set foot on that island—two journalists who had prepared for the visit by taking a survival course! The trade winds blow incessantly on Necker, which measures 74 acres, and the little black sand flies savour succulent human flesh. When Richard bought the island, there was no fresh water, no electricity, no drainage and certainly nowhere to land a boat, much less a plane. Yes, he was accustomed to challenges but this one surely seemed insurmountable.

On the day we arrived, the clouds gathered and the heavens opened up. The turquoise sea gained momentum as our yacht tipped and rolled with Joe at the wheel and Woody as skipper, who was leaping back and forth to check that all was lashed down. This stormy crossing from Virgin Gorda took 40 minutes; it seemed as though it was the nature gods' last plea to keep humans away from this uncultivated piece of land.

With Woody's experience and charts at the ready, he managed to guide us through the only approach, a narrow opening in the coral reef surrounding the island. Inside there were only two boats, one belonging to divers from a neighbouring island and a yacht full of passengers who were picnicking on one of the sandy coves.

CHAPTER 5

The nature gods finally gave up whilst we lowered anchor and the sun came out and stayed with us for the rest of the day. We watched a giant ray flapping its way serenely along the sandy sea bottom. Nesting gulls and terns screeched, whilst pelicans fished in formation above. The island had two long sandy beaches, one east and one west. We chose to anchor off the west beach where we clambered into the dinghy and managed to glide gracefully to shore on a wave.

We changed into our sturdy shoes, donned long trousers, put on gloves and delved into the prickly undergrowth to try to hike to the island's highest point. We accomplished this with some difficulty, as every known cactus pierced us, even penetrating our shoes, shirts and trousers. But we made it to the top, scaring the odd goat in our path. Joe was the only one to give up, which was understandable, given that he had the misfortune to sit on a prickly pear! For the rest of us, the climb was worth it, for the view of all 44 Virgin Islands was breathtaking. Surely this would be the perfect place for a house.

Necker was far larger than we had imagined and was divided by two saltwater lakes and sandy beaches. We couldn't wait for Richard to join us so we could report what we'd discovered on our exploratory hike. Animal and bird life was plentiful: we saw hummingbirds, lizards and large yellow and black caterpillars stopping in their tracks with inquisitive expressions as if to say, "What the hell are you doing here?" No doubt the wild goats gazing up from the small valley below had also been getting along very happily without us.

In spite of crunching land crabs underfoot, we found the descent easier and took a quick swim to wash away all the prickles and blood before lunch revived us. Ted had suggested I take off my wedding ring whilst swimming, as the glitter might attract barracudas. I obeyed, but alas, I was never to see it again—to this day, I imagine my ring is still buried somewhere deep in the sand around Necker.

We decided it would be better to explore the other side of the island by dinghy. As we rowed over a garden of sea fans, sponges, parrotfish, ilk horn and brain coral, the deep clear water showcased a sparkling portrait of the underwater world.

The next beach was a natural paradise with every type of coral imaginable. "Just how could we take some of it home?" asked Ted. "Leave it where it belongs!" was my reply. But eventually we compromised on the matter and Woody would discover us late that night with a dinghy half-full of our beach finds. Thank goodness for a good-natured skipper!

It's amazing how contented five people can be, spending a whole morning in a very small cockpit without another soul around, for this is what we did, still anchored off West Bay. To the north, there was a steep rocky drop into rough, inky blue seas, giving six white long-tailed Pacific birds a perfect background.

That afternoon, we would set out to explore another vista. After a steep walk up to the hilltop, with sand crabs underfoot, we found a stack of small boulders, no doubt left by Richard on his first visit. Our delight in finding a tree alive with hummingbirds was tempered by our "ow's" and "oo's" as we all stepped on lethal prickly cacti that pierced even my golfing shoes. Joe was pricked simultaneously in both feet and I managed to prevent him from sitting on yet another cactus. This surely was the very last cry from the nature gods: "Leave Necker alone, you Homo sapiens!"

We decided to leave the northwest corner for another day and, after a hazardous prickly descent, we all plunged once more into the sea—what a relief! We felt we deserved a special dinner that night, so Jackie and Woody produced a charcoal chicken feast that we eagerly devoured under the light of a pierced coconut with a candle flickering inside.

✈

On the eighth day of our journey, we arrived at Virgin Gorda and enjoyed a four-course breakfast, complete with champagne, at the Bitter End Yacht Club. The following morning we pulled up anchor and sailed the length of Tortola, past Little Hatch, Great Hatch and many other small islands. When we anchored in American waters off St. Thomas, Jackie and I sent the boys ashore to fetch Richard while we prepared a dinner of the kingfish we'd caught on Necker. We had just completed the preparations when we heard a boat engine approaching and the sound of laughter from Ted, Richard and Joe. Surprise, surprise! They were carrying six large glasses frothing over with banana daiquiris, which they'd toted all the way from a bar on an island nearby. Amidst much bawdy laughter, we all enjoyed our drinks followed by fish, caviar and wine. There would be no trouble sleeping soundly that night!

After 12 days out, we had every intention of doing some intense exploration of Necker, deciding to circle it once to take photographs from all angles and to check out the safest approaches. We managed to find a gap in the reef on the northeast side and made a slow approach, anchoring off the southwest corner. The sun was blazing as we packed up the dinghy with all our exploring gear plus the usual sail bag full of flippers, goggles, cameras, golfing shoes, trousers, bathing costumes and lots of food. We waved goodbye to Woody who, quite rightly, would not leave the yacht, as the swell was strong and the waves were pounding the beach.

Landing safely on the beach, Ted, Richard and I decided to swim out to the reef. After seeing a barracuda, I decided to stay close to Ted! Richard shouted to us to look below at a shoal of about 50 deep blue fish, their fins sparkling in the bright sunlight. We must have seen 200 species of coral before we returned to shore for lunch under the shade of a sea-vine.

While preparing lunch, Jackie and I heard a shout from Richard: "Come quickly! We've just seen a shark!" In our haste to see the shark, we forgot about the land crabs that, in our absence, must have thoroughly enjoyed a good portion of our beautifully set-out lunch.

After eating what was left of our meal, we set out to explore again, by now well aware of the merciless cacti. We were entranced when we spied a large dried-up lake framed with mango trees and romantic sandy paths, none of which were visible from the water. My mind boggled at the potential of this fairy tale island. Jackie, a sculptor, was beside herself as she dug away, finding a substance she described as porcelain clay.

We had yet to explore Necker's northwest corner. It was so hot that we decided to take the dinghy to unload some of our gear on the yacht and pick up more cold drinks before landing on the west beach. As Woody handed us juice and beer, he remarked that we seemed to have a heavier load than when we started. This we soon regretted, as we were pounded by big waves and Jackie shouted (too late) that there were rocks ahead. Over we went with Jackie now crying, "My camera!"

Richard was laughing as he reached out to help Joe, who—unable to swim—was hanging onto the capsized boat. I imagined being marooned forever on this wild island. We swam about madly, retrieving oars, bailer, shoes and oranges. Oh, the thought of Necker without shoes!

Before long, all was recovered and we pulled the dinghy onto the beach, where we quietly nursed our various wounds. The sun was getting low as we discussed launching that dinghy with the possibility of the engine not working, given the fact that Joe could not swim. After a confab, we decided that Richard would swim with the boat out to sea beyond the worst waves and then climb aboard, whilst we walked with all the gear back over the rocks on the south point to the more peaceful east side where Richard would pick us all up.

And so, as the sun was setting, Woody received a somewhat bedraggled little party, slightly ashamed of their foolishness but thankful that no one was hurt and that Ted's camera was still dry!

✈

The following day Richard suggested that we might all learn to scuba dive. His determination took him off in the dinghy earlier than usual, returning two hours later to announce that he had scheduled diving for that afternoon at Little Dix Bay. He would not join us, as he had to catch a plane at 3pm, due to urgent work he had to tend to in the States.

He was packed in five minutes, dressed in smart clothes in another five minutes and then was gone. Meanwhile, we headed over to Gun Creek for our scuba lessons. While I had no experience, Ted had already been trained in scuba in England with Vanessa at the Paddington swimming pool, so he had his "paddy" licence. We were both nervous, though, as we were given our first few instructions in the back of the launch. Jackie remarked that she had heart trouble and a hearing problem and she, too, was worried.

Having donned our masks, weights and bottles, we all had a limited training session in shallow water. Before there was time to chicken out, we were herded back to the launch and proceeded full speed out to sea. What price then to leap overboard! Fear is a nasty, prickly thing.

When we finally stopped and the anchor line was thrown over, we were told that we had nothing to fear; we were going to dive only 40 feet. Only 40? We were all quite terrified and sat unmoving on the end of the launch until I was instructed to go first and was firmly pushed from behind, having only sufficient time to send up a quick prayer. Splash! I was in and sinking fast, mask having gone askew and in my panic, forgetting all I had been told.

There was nothing left to do but join the others down below. Pulling myself together, I started to descend, clutching at the rope, trying to make my ears pop every foot until the pressure seemed too great and hastily I surfaced again. This I repeated four or five times like a yoyo and each time I surfaced, I saw the instructor shouting at Jackie. Finally, I could not bear to see her being bullied any more so I shouted up, spluttering through my mask, "Don't do it Jackie, you'll hurt your ears!" Again I sank, as my weights pulled me back down.

This time I ascended even faster. Why I wasn't better monitored to prevent my descent and rapid ascent, I'll never know. I later learned that if I had held my breath going up, I could have blown a hole in my lungs! Ted, meanwhile, was having a fine time at the bottom, accompanied by the lead instructor. It was only when he saw his wife bobbing up and down that he surfaced and cajoled me down to touch the sea bed. Although I was finding it hard to stay down, I was able to relax sufficiently to note the wonderland of corals, fishes and fantastic colours.

After everyone was safely back on the launch, the instructor asked why I didn't have any weights on. They must have come off at the bottom—it was no wonder I could not stay down! Finally, our group of scuba divers-in-training was whisked back to Little Dix Bay, some of them determined to try again. I had mixed feelings, but at least I felt that I had not let Richard down.

✈

That evening Ted and I took a romantically lit path to a beautifully situated hotel with a world of taste and elegance within. The couple running the hotel, Libby and Jorgen Tronning, had met Richard and were very keen to help him with his island project. After seeing Necker in its present state, they weren't sure it was possible to make it habitable, but if anyone could do it, Jorgen said Richard was the person.

Ted and I spent a wonderful hour taking another scuba lesson the next morning, this time with a kind young instructor named Chip. During the dive, as we explored the sea bed around the island, he pointed out the dreaded fire coral and long-tailed sea urchins, tickled a lobster's tentacles and picked up a spider crab.

Chip pointed out the wreck of a 19th century ship that had been sheltering from a hurricane when she dragged her anchor and all were lost. We swam up to the porthole to watch many small fish enjoying their own investigation of the coral-encrusted wreck.

At the last porthole, a big grouper, with eyes larger and wider than mine, suddenly confronted me. I am not sure who was the more frightened but Ted, close behind, thought it was a fine joke as I scrambled to the surface, glad to return to the safety of land.

The next day, after two weeks of the most pleasurable exploration, we sadly left our yacht and let the ramshackle bus jog us over the rough, hilly road to Trellis Bay Airport to catch our plane home.

CHAPTER 6

B Y 1981 WE WERE THE proud grandparents of three children: Lindy's two sons, Jack and Ned, ages one and three, and Richard and Joan's daughter, Holly, who was born in November of that year. It was a busy but happy time for the family. During the week, Ted and I lived in our little flat in London and each weekend we'd pack up and go to Tanyards. I had bought a double canoe, so on summer evenings after work we would strap it to the top of our old car and drive down to Putney to launch it and row down the Thames. We'd stop off at pubs along the way and then catch the tide and return home, with only the swans for company.

✈

One morning we got a phone call from Richard. "Mum, Dad, I've just bought an old barge in Oxford. Would you like to bring it down the Thames so I can put it next to my houseboat? Business is looking good and I could use more space."

It sounded like a fun idea and we thought we could handle it. A hasty pack of old clothes and enough food for the week and we sped off to Oxford. There we met the man who'd sold Richard the barge at the local gate at Kidlington. Behind him was one of the widest, largest barges I'd ever seen. In days gone by it had carried coal down the Thames to London. My heart sank. Would we really be able to get it down the Thames to Little Venice? Ted was confident that we could manage it, so off we chugged.

We seemed to be doing fine until we reached the second lock. With no prior experience of the process, we approached the lock far too fast. Ted shouted, "Quick, Eve, tie up to the bollard," whilst he frantically tried to get the boat into reverse. The ratchels were old and rusty and not capable of stopping this heavy old coal barge, which was fast approaching the lock gate. Leaping ashore, I tied the ropes around the bollard. By now, Ted was reversing, which caused the rope to tighten, trapping my right hand. In a panic, rather than have my whole body get caught, I pulled my hand loose, leaving my fingers a bloody, mangled mess.

Thankfully my first aid training from the war days came back to me: "Reach land, lie down, and treat for shock and bleeding." I managed to hurry across the lock planks and made it to land, but I don't remember much else besides thinking, "There goes my right hand! No more writing, tennis, golf or playing the piano!" Ted somehow got me to the nearest hospital and within minutes Richard arrived, assuring me he'd find the best surgeon in London, which, bless him, he did. After a few operations, though my hand was not very attractive, I was using it again, even playing tennis and golf, but left with a convenient excuse not to play the piano, which I'm sure was a relief to the family!

✈

In the summer of 1983, I was busy preparing for Vanessa's wedding to Robert Devereux. This was to be my Tanyards swan song, the wedding of my youngest child. Every year a travelling fair came to Shamley Green and luckily I'd become friendly with the owner. So I asked him if I could rent his entire fair for the evening wedding party and he gladly obliged. The result was a fancy costume party and circus, all in one. Some of the costumes worn by the guests were hilarious, although they caused a spot of bother when our postman, arriving early the next morning, saw a tiger wandering home and promptly crossed to the other side of the road!

CHAPTER 6

At the wedding my Colts team held bats high as Robert and Vanessa emerged from the village church, with Vanessa wearing her great, great, great grandmother's wedding dress and looking radiant. Afterward, at the evening circus party, I decided to let my hair down and dressed as a trapeze artist in black fishnet tights and mask. Who would recognise the bride's mother anyway? Some of the family didn't think it was quite proper but it was my last family wedding, after all. We all had a wow of an evening, with Richard dressed up as the ringleader, last seen chasing a monkey over the Big Top!

✈

When your last child gets married and the party's over, it's easy to succumb to depression, which I did. I felt miserable. So I decided to buy a caravan and forget my gloom with some travelling. Ted was dead against it, which I could later understand! We did make one trip to Wales but we never even managed to square the caravan on a sloping field. What with Ted's gin and tonic sliding hither and thither, we decided this would be the last time we took the caravan on the road, and indeed it was. You can't win 'em all!

✈

With the children gone, there seemed to be no reason to continue living in Surrey. Richard and Lindy seldom visited Shamley Green anymore. Richard had his Virgin business to run and Lindy, who was now on her own, was busy raising her two boys. Vanessa was also busy running her gallery on Portobello Road. That's when I decided to buy a home by the sea to lure the family down for weekends.

Ted was just beginning to enjoy an early retirement but my mind was made up—the time had come for a change! Every free weekend I would drive two hours to visit the West Wittering area to reassure myself that it would be the ideal place to live, not only for Ted's retirement but also for me, with tennis, golf and sailing nearby. Ted agreed that I might look for a house but was adamant that he would not move unless I managed to find a house similar to Tanyards. Brown envelope after brown envelope arrived in the mail, but no house for sale seemed similar to ours.

One day, just as we were leaving for Menorca, another brown envelope arrived. The property for sale was Cakeham Manor, a 13th century farmhouse with some of its walls still made out of wattle and daub—just the sort of place that would satisfy Ted.

From the 13th through the 16th centuries, it was the summer palace of the bishops of Chichester. Still standing on the property was a lofty, hexagonal, crenelated brick tower with a winding staircase leading up to the top, where one could see views of the harbour and beyond, even to the Isle of Wight. Halfway up the tower was a watchman's room, still intact, and below the tower, a portion of the original chapel remained.

The tower was used to watch for ships from the Spanish Armada and in the Napoleonic era, when there was a great threat of invasion, to allow relays of coast guards to keep watch. On hearing that in 1245, Saint Richard of Wynch performed miracles at Cakeham, we knew this was the place for us.

Cakeham Manor was about to be auctioned so I made a hasty phone call to Richard, leaving a message asking him to bid for us. Off we flew to Menorca without hearing a word back from him. So I bid by telephone, and after several tense rounds of bidding, with Lindy urging me forward, I won the auction at £48,000. That seemed high, but little did I know that Richard had indeed received my message and he was the unnamed opponent bidding against me!

✈

My delight at my good fortune was short-lived, as the year 1984 was a disastrous one to be selling a house. Share prices were tumbling along with the property market. We hoped to sell Tanyards, complete with cottage and barns, and put it all into Cakeham, which was in a derelict state. But there were very few buyers interested in Tanyards. Just what had I done?

Against all odds, we finally found a buyer, a man who said he wanted to purchase the house for his new bride. We learned later that he was a developer and were disappointed to hear that he divided up our family home into several units. Still, we were happy to have made enough on the sale to pay for the move and the renovations to Cakeham. I had been wishing for a change and I'd certainly achieved my goal!

It was sad when we said our final goodbye to Tanyards, our beloved old farmhouse, and made the move to Cakeham Manor. After three decades in the same home, the scope of such a move seemed monumental. Ted cleared the barns of load after load of wood as I packed countless boxes with our possessions.

After three days of unpacking at Cakeham, I locked the door, got into the car and sped back to Tanyards for a last look around. A nasty lump stuck in my throat on seeing the empty shell, the home that had served our family so well.

Memories came surging back as I recalled the wonderful parties we'd had around the swimming pool. Yes, Tanyards held many wonderful memories, but it was time to move on. Ted and I had already visited the Red Lion in Shamley Green to say goodbye to all the friends we'd made over the years and to introduce them to the new owners of Tanyards. At times like that, I tend to remind myself how important it is never to dwell on the past when there's always a future to look forward to.

Before long, we would manage to make the wattle and daub manor house habitable. We created a hard tennis court, sorted out a neglected walled garden and added a duck pond to the property. The house came alive on the weekends with our grandchildren and their friends; they all loved the old tower and ruined chapel below and happily followed our path to the sandy beach that was only a five-minute walk from the house.

WINDSURF ADVENTURE

Our family seemed intent on new challenges. This time it was up to Robin Brockway, our future son-in-law, a graphic designer and calligrapher who had kindly reached out to me when he heard from a colleague about my boating accident. Though we had never met, he sent me writing exercises every few days during my early recovery, which I practiced eagerly each time I heard from him. When we finally did meet in person, I thanked him for giving me hope when I thought might never be able to write longhand again. When he told me he was a windsurfer, I invited him to Menorca to visit and to windsurf, as it was a great spot for that. On his first visit he met Lindy, and I was happy to think that I was the one who brought them together.

Robin shared our family's spirit of adventure. Before long he told us he was being sponsored by a ferry company to be the first windsurfer to race a ferry across the English Channel, from Ramsgate to Dunkirk. Lindy and I went along on the ferry, together with the press and photographers, whilst Robin left Ramsgate with only a wetsuit, flares and a rubber support boat with a change of sails, should he need them on his 34-mile journey.

All was fine for the first two hours but the support boat, which was carrying a journalist from the *Daily Express*, couldn't keep up with the speed Robin was making. Robin lost sight of the boat, as he wished to change his sail in a wind force 9 that had blown up. Before long, not knowing where he was, he stopped in the middle of the shipping lane for over an hour, waiting for the boat to catch up. Floating in the water, surrounded by huge tankers, he began to wonder if his adventure was worth the risk.

But there was no time for regret: it was getting dark, so he used his flares and was finally picked up by the support boat, much to the relief of the journalist, whose complexion was changing rapidly from yellow to green. Meanwhile Lindy and I had returned to Ramsgate on the ferry wondering where on earth Robin was heading. There was much happiness all around when he finally turned up on the beach at Ramsgate—wet and exhausted but determined to try again.

A few months later, unbeknownst to anyone but two of his friends, Robin left on his windsurfer from Ramsgate, this time without a support boat. Though it took eight and a half hours, he arrived after dark in Dunkirk, where he walked into a restaurant on the beach. When the French owner heard Robin had just windsurfed across the channel, he threw up his hands and said, "You English are mad!"

Robin had not broken a record but he had accomplished his goal, which was more important to him in the long run. When his friends finally arrived, they found Robin in the disco under the restaurant, dancing in his wetsuit. It was a well-deserved celebration indeed!

THE VIRGIN INAUGURAL

Ted and I were surprised when Richard called to tell us that he'd made a special announcement at a Virgin staff meeting, saying he was thinking about starting an airline, one that would provide travellers with both better service and lower prices for transatlantic flights. He said he was met with gasps of disbelief: leave it to British Airways or People's Express, his staff pleaded. But Richard knew what he wanted, and in June 1984, the first Virgin Atlantic Boeing 747 was ready for its test flight.

The only journalist covering that flight was from the *Financial Times*. All went well that day until the plane lurched to the left and a massive flame shot out of one engine, followed by a long trail of black smoke and stunned silence from those on board. The engines were uninsured so the end of Virgin Atlantic airlines could have happened that day, before it was even launched. Instead, there was relief all round when the plane landed safely and the cause of the explosion was identified as a flock of birds that had been sucked into one engine. The journalist was sporting and didn't run the story. If he had, who knows if Virgin Atlantic would exist today!

Still, the unfortunate incident stood in the way of the licence Richard needed to be approved before the first flight between London and New York, which was scheduled for three days hence. All the family was planning to be aboard this grand inaugural flight, so throughout the day we were constantly phoning each other, wondering what would happen.

The night of the test flight, we gathered at Richard's new London house on Oxford Road, waiting anxiously for his return. He and Joan were due to dine at 10 Downing Street with Prime Minister Margaret Thatcher in just one hour, but there was no sign of him.

Joan, well used to these last-minute panics, was peacefully getting ready while Holly, now two years old, raced around the large, nearly empty house, her giggles keeping everyone amused. Suddenly crash, bang! The front door flew open and Richard dashed in. Panting, he announced that only five minutes earlier his American licence had been granted. He struggled into his dinner jacket, bought off the peg only that day. It fitted him well, but only in the nick of time did we notice the price tag hanging out of his collar! Already late, we bundled into my Honda and I chauffeured them at top speed to 10 Downing Street. He and Joan arrived ten minutes late, but I'm sure Mrs. Thatcher understood, once she discovered the reason!

In a short period, Richard had found an aircraft, obtained licences, hired staff and had designer uniforms made for the flight crew and employees. And now here we were on board! Was it really happening? Would we actually get off the ground? Many such questions were running through our heads as the 747 taxied down the runway on Friday, 22 June 1984.

It was an exciting and proud day for me and Ted. The send-off at Gatwick had been tremendous, with a seething mass of press and television cameras everywhere. Being amongst the first to board the plane, we had a first-class view of the crowd on the tarmac surging forward as Richard appeared.

It was a spectacle indeed, with the old brass band playing a joyful tune while Richard, holding Holly in his arms, ran up the steps to the plane, champagne bottle in hand. In spite of all this excitement he remembered to give it a good shake before releasing the cork. The cheers grew louder from the excited crowd below as he poured champagne over the magnificent red and white aircraft called the Maiden Voyager.

The cabin crew opened all the cabin doors as the crowd on the tarmac shouted and applauded. However, there was no chance the aircraft would leave on schedule; it was 25 minutes late for take-off by the time the last passengers boarded. The flight attendants, all smartly dressed in their grey and red uniforms, were equally excited and nervous on this first Virgin Atlantic Flight 001.

The pressure and tension during the last few days had been enormous, even for the always-optimistic Rick. (I was the only one who was allowed to call him Rick or Ricky—that was my special right as his mother! To the rest of the world, he would always be Richard.)

Now we were ready to go. On board, the excitement was building as champagne was passed all around. Once seatbelts were secured, the pilot's voice came over the speaker loud and clear: "Since this is our first flight, we thought you might like to share our view from the flight deck and see what really happens when we take off."

All eyes were glued to the overhead video screen as we watched the runway stretched out in front of us. As the plane gathered speed and the tarmac began to rush by beneath the windscreen, we noticed that the pilots looked unusually relaxed. Rather than staring intently ahead and flying the plane, they were looking sideways at each other and smiling. Here we were hurtling down the runway and the pilots appeared not to be paying attention!

There was a deathly hush as the nose of the plane rose up and the runway began to disappear from view. At this moment, we saw one of the pilots pull out a marijuana cigarette and offer it to his co-pilot. All hearts stopped until the two pilots then took off their caps and turned around to face the camera. They were none other than the famous cricketers Ian Botham and Viv Richards, along with Richard posing as the flight engineer. Everyone on board laughed, relieved to realize this was yet another of Richard's jokes. We learned later that the video had been filmed the previous day on a flight simulator.

When we reached altitude, Richard moved through the plane, chatting up the passengers and the press on board. The few paying passengers seemed thrilled to be on this inaugural flight, with champagne corks popping. To make the six and a half hour flight even more enjoyable, Virgin had hired the magician Simon Drake to perform his tricks and the amazing East End singers, The Mint Julep, to entertain us all with their a cappella singing.

Soon the flight turned into a glorious cocktail party. The good-natured flight attendants didn't seem to mind the excited passengers, including my 86-year-old mother, moving up and down the aisles to chat and drink with their friends. As the passengers became more exuberant, crowding around the bar, the captain's only hope of getting them to sit down for the four-course lunch from Maxim's was to announce that we were about to encounter turbulence so everyone must be seated, with seatbelts fastened.

The flight ended with a safe and smooth landing at Newark Airport outside of New York City, cheered on by all 450 passengers on board. It was a happy occasion until Richard realised he had forgotten his passport. In spite of this, the American authorities graciously allowed him to enter the country!

CHAPTER 7

I'S NOT OFTEN THAT I board a plane without knowing why or where I am going. But in February 1985, Ted and I walked up the steps of Richard's new Virgin Atlantic plane, accompanied by a group of equally bemused journalists. A couple of weeks earlier, a strange invitation had dropped through our mail slot. It read: "Ted and Eve Branson are invited to the airborne launch of one of the major international challenges of 1985. Venue: somewhere over the Atlantic, 6 February 1985." We were asked to keep the whole business a secret, which wasn't difficult, given that we had absolutely no idea what it was all about. We could only wait and see.

With his sudden launch of an airline, we were getting used to Richard's surprises. Once we were high above the Atlantic on the day of this escapade, we learned more. The video screens flickered to life and the lights were dimmed. Everyone fell silent as a deep, theatrical voice came over the speakers to say that the original Blue Riband was an honour bestowed upon a ship in regular passenger service that made a westbound crossing of the Atlantic Ocean with the record highest speed.

Everyone looked surprised and shuffled in their seats, preparing themselves for the kicker. I think Ted and I sensed what was coming.

Looking out the window below us, we knew the Atlantic held a certain fascination for Richard. Crossing it by air in his jumbo jet just wasn't enough.

The commentator went on to explain that the Blue Riband title had passed through the hands of many nations until the present holder, the SS United States, claimed it on her maiden voyage in 1952. Since that date, no vessel had challenged her until today. The Virgin Atlantic Challenger would attempt to win back the Blue Riband for Great Britain.

A spontaneous cheer swept through the cabin. We then learned that in 1935, the Hales trophy was donated by a British Member of Parliament who owned a shipping company, Harold K. Hales, as the prize representing the Blue Riband title. He changed the rules slightly by saying that the trophy would be awarded to the passenger ship making the fastest Atlantic crossing in either direction. The trophy itself is a magnificent, four-foot statue made of gold-plated solid silver and mounted on an onyx base, weighing nearly 100 pounds; it had been housed in the New York Maritime Museum for the past 34 years.

Not for much longer, I thought. Richard caught my eye and smiled. All this talk of awards was taking me back to when we used to attend summer sports days at his school. Today he had that same relaxed, nonchalant look he had as a boy. His achievements always come across as cavalier and effortless. During the month before, when he was launching the airline, for example, it had all seemed so lighthearted and casual. It wasn't, of course, nor was this latest venture, despite the smile. The commentator continued:

"In the 14 years between the inaugural title challenge in 1938 and the SS United States' victory in 1952, there were no fewer than 87 successful British challenges. Famous vessels such as the Lusitania, the Mauritania and the Queen Mary were involved. In fact, during the 1930s, the Blue Riband became such a matter of national pride that vast fortunes were spent on winning the coveted prize. Many nations competed. Italy held it for a while, at the insistence of Mussolini, who had Rex, a giant liner, specially built for the challenge."

CHAPTER 7

With a team of eight, Richard planned to leave from the Ambrose Light station in New York Bay and follow a route that would take advantage of the prevailing wind pattern. Their goal was to make the trip in three days and three nights and knock ten hours off the record.

As soon as the video ended, reporters and cameramen from the main lounge dashed up the narrow staircase to our cabin where we sat with the crew members who were about to take part in this dangerous, gruelling task. It was time for interviews.

Richard had assembled the top people in their fields to join him on the challenge. The skipper would be powerboat racer Ted Toleman and first mate would be none other than Scottish yachtsman Chay Blyth, a good choice indeed. Chay's first heroic feat was rowing across the Atlantic in an open dory in 1966. Not content with that, in 1971 Chay was the first to sail around the world, going from east to west against the prevailing winds and currents. Now he was game to help Richard beat the speed record across the Atlantic.

They chose Dag Pike as their navigator, a position responsible not only for avoiding floating icebergs and debris but also for manoeuvring in the fog. With an art image intensifier and his 40-odd years of navigational experience, it seemed likely that all would be well. Other members of the crew were Steve Ridgway, Project Manager; "Nobby" Clarke, Chief Mechanic; and Peter Macann, who would be filming the challenge for the BBC.

According to the Blue Riband rules, there also had to be a fare-paying passenger on board, a role that would conveniently fall to Richard! Somehow I couldn't quite picture him as just a passenger; I had no doubt he would take his turn at the helm.

By now the Virgin 747 was circling over the Scilly Isles. The pilot dipped one wing to point out the finishing goal, the Bishop's Rock Lighthouse. I could just imagine the face of the lighthouse keeper looking up, wondering what on earth the jumbo jet was doing, screeching low over his head.

✈

Four months later, the entire Branson family, from my mother down to our newest member, Lindy and Robin's infant son Otto, assembled at Buckler's Yard Hotel in Beaulieu to witness the naming ceremony and launch of the Challenger.

The following day we set off early to Cougar Marine Yard on the Hamble River and queued up with hundreds of other cars. Seeing a grandstand and vast reception tent added to my trepidation about what lay ahead for Richard as well as for us.

The area soon filled up with press and onlookers. The national anthem sounded as the patrons and Prince and Princess Michael of Kent arrived to take their positions on the grandstand. Suddenly three-year-old Holly freed herself from Joan's care and rushed onto the platform to be with her father. Much to the crowd's delight, she failed to understand why she shouldn't be allowed up there too. Princess Michael named the boat with the obligatory bottle of champagne and amidst cheers and an uplifting rendition of Rule Britannia, the Virgin Atlantic Challenger gracefully slipped off into the Hamble.

Two weeks later, we were invited to the Challenger's first sea trials and found ourselves visiting the boatyard to have a proper look at the boat. Painted pale red and gray, it had a look of quiet confidence about it, but I wanted to know exactly how a 65-foot catamaran was going to survive the trip, particularly travelling at such high speeds. I asked our guide why the boat was made of aluminium and not wood or fibreglass. I was told that aluminium allowed the boat to be sufficiently light to travel at high speed while being tough enough to withstand the pummelling that would be meted out by the Atlantic.

Now my heartbeat ceased being regular. I wanted to cry out, "Call it a day, Rick," but I knew it was unwise to interfere.

Glistening in the sun, the propellers were clearly the highlight of the craft; they were also its most vulnerable feature. Should they get entangled with debris, Peter Macann, a trained diver, would have to abandon his camera, hop overboard, and fit the spare set.

Inside the wheelhouse, I looked around in vain for signs of domestic comfort. Not only was there no galley but there were only two bunks and two reclining seats for the off-duty crewmembers. Where were the loos? I suppose the spare pair of propellers had to take priority.

✈

CHAPTER 7

When we returned to the Cougar shipyard tem days later, it was quite deserted. Gone were the waving flags, the bustling stands and the marquees from the day of the boat's christening. No band played as we made our way down to the water's edge where we found the Challenger lying peacefully on her mooring. Now we would be able to truly inspect and experience this 65-footer before she took her sea trials.

It was an easy job casting off and we were soon gliding along the Hamble River. Ted Toleman was keen to put her two 2,000-horsepower diesel engines through their paces around the Isle of Wight after three years of working on her design. The SS United States had won the Blue Riband with a 240,000-horse power engine, the size of a small cathedral. We could all feel the raw energy barely held in check as Ted reluctantly abided by the five-knot speed limit in the harbour.

Once in the Solent, we planed gracefully across pond-like conditions, people waving and cheering as we passed. The ride was smooth and exhilarating, quite different, I imagined, from how the Atlantic would feel. We circled the Isle of Wight in a matter of minutes and stopped at Cowes Harbour for tea. Our arrival caused quite a stir, as no one had ever seen anything quite like the Challenger, even amongst the Cowes yachtics.

We left the harbour feeling rather smug, too smug as it turned out. As we entered the Hamble, a plume of coal-black smoke billowed from the engines, totally enveloping a yacht we had just passed. Moments earlier, the yacht's captain had been cheering us on. Our engineer promptly shut down the engines and announced that we had blown a gasket.

Embarrassed, we were unceremoniously towed back up the Hamble by the harbour master. All the boats we had overtaken now overtook us, their captains sportingly looking in the other direction. Thank God it was only a trial run!

✈

The Challenger was soon transported to America and on 18 July 1985, we received a rather plaintive telephone call from Richard, who was in America too. It was his birthday but he didn't sound very celebratory. A hurricane was blowing and fog had descended over the Atlantic. And there was more: the icebergs were the worst ever reported. If Richard's crew managed to keep south by 42 degrees latitude, they would just be able to avoid them. The crossing had been pushed back three days. If only it were three years! His tone was very bleak and I wondered if he really knew what he was in for. In spite of choosing the top sailors and engineers, there were many treacherous obstacles ahead.

Ted and I were on the Isle of Wight, watching the final days of Cowes Week, where boats of every conceivable shape and size battled a choppy Solent en route to Ireland. This was a poignant and timely reminder to us of how dangerous the sea can be.

On our return home, we heard a message from Richard on the answerphone: "Hi Mum, Dad, tried to phone you on the Isle of Wight, but no answer. Just to say we're off in the morning and, by the way, I love you both."

It sounded ominous. Richard wasn't given to open expressions of love like that. He must have suffered pangs, thinking of what lay ahead and what he'd left behind—Joan was pregnant with their second child. But the venture would go on, regardless; we learned from Joan that the Challenger would leave at four in the morning the next day.

✈

The following day started innocently enough, with breakfast at home with Lindy, Robin, Ned, Jack and little Otto. Suddenly things began to happen. The telephone rang with the news that Joan had gone into labour and was being rushed off to the hospital. Our dilemma was getting the news to Richard. Just as I was about to pick up the phone to contact Richard's team, it rang again; the Challenger had crossed the starting line. Too late! Just as well, I thought. He had more than enough on his mind.

For the next few hours I was on the phone nonstop to the project's personnel coordinator in London. He arranged for all of us to fly to the Scilly Isles and, if the Challenger was successful, back to London for a heady round of receptions. It had also been agreed that the boat would be taken up the Thames if they beat the record.

CHAPTER 7

As I packed up the family to head to London, a phone call came through from Joan, who had wonderful news of the birth of a seven-pound baby, Sam. She asked if I could get the message through to Richard. Of course I would, even if it meant swimming out to tell him!

I drove madly down Oxford Street to the Virgin Megastore and rushed upstairs to operation headquarters. Everyone was dressed in red and white Virgin overalls. The ground crew was monitoring the Challenger's progress with the help of ship-to-shore telex. At the far end of the room, the public relations team was coordinating all the information and sending it out in a nonstop stream of press releases. Ever the good hosts, they were also manning a bar for the team and any curious members of the public who strolled in off the street.

Every hour on the hour, the Challenger made radio contact with the operations team. At exactly 8pm, the hotline telephone buzzed to life. Tim Powell, the project coordinator, talked directly to Chay Blyth, who was now speaking from the middle of the Atlantic.

"Chay, is Richard awake? Over."

"Yes. Over."

"I've got his mother here with an important message. Over."

Tim passed the phone over to me. The line was muffled. I could hear the incessant roar of the engines in the background. "Hi, Richard," I shouted. "You're a proud dad. Over."

"What did you say?" he shouted back.

"You are a proud father," I repeated. "It's a fine Blue Riband baby. Over."

"Boy or girl? Over."

"Blue is for boys, you fool. Over."

There was a pause and then, "Whooppee!"

I shouted back, "Come home quickly!"

"I'm coming as fast as I can, Mum."

Feeling much better now that Richard knew the good news, I passed the receiver back to Tim Powell, who was back to business with technical details from the ground crew. The last message, though, was from Richard, who sent his love to Joan. He said the Challenger crew would open their only bottle of champagne, which had originally been intended for the finish.

By the following day, the news of Richard and Joan's baby was all over the tabloid newspapers. The timely birth had given the media a wonderful angle on the Challenger, but it had created a few problems as well. We went to see Joan at the London hospital, where many reporters were trying to interview her. I spent most of the morning keeping them at bay. As for Sam, he was a beautiful baby and just like Richard, strong-willed!

It felt as though the whole country swelled with excitement about the Challenger. TV and radio bulletins regularly reported her progress across the Atlantic. Still, we couldn't help ringing up the Megastore every hour or so to hear about the crew's progress from the ops room. At one point they ran into a shoal of whales, but the first refuelling went better than expected. And they were well ahead of schedule, averaging 42 knots.

At 6.30am the following day, we collected Lindy and her two eldest sons, Jack and Ned, now five and seven. It was comforting to have the family together in times like this. One can only hope the boys were old enough to remember those exciting days.

We had been listening to the radio bulletins on the journey but had heard nothing to prepare us for the news awaiting us at Plymouth's tiny airport. A Virgin project manager was there to greet us.

"The news is bad," he whispered to me. "I am telling you, but for now, please don't let other relatives of the crew know. They have been through a night of pretty bad weather, up to force seven gales, although Chay sounded cheery enough. He said it was good for his figure."

I suddenly felt a wave of guilt for encouraging Richard to be so adventurous when he was growing up. I told Ted the news. We both felt uneasy and slightly isolated, not being able to share our worries with the other families.

By 9.30am more bad news came. One of the engines was leaking and they could only average 35 knots. At 11am, before contact was lost, the report had indicated very bad weather. That was all we knew as we boarded a twin-engine plane bound for the Scilly Isles.

By 12.15pm, an RAF Nimrod left St. Morgans, near St. Ives, expecting to guide the refuelling ship for a rendezvous with the Challenger. Their estimated time of arrival at the Scilly Isles was 7.30pm the following evening after three solid days of the sea's relentless pounding and the deafening noise and constant vibration of the engine.

They had covered more than 3,000 miles with the Hales Trophy inspiring them; now their reward was close at hand. To beat the record, they had to reach Bishop's Rock Lighthouse before 10.02pm. All I wanted by this point was news that they were safe. Why, oh, why did we raise such a fearless boy?

There was a problem finding accommodations on Scilly for all of us, for we had arrived at the height of tourist season. The kind -hearted islanders came to our rescue, giving up spare bedrooms and supplying camp beds. The next day, Ted, Lindy, Ned, Jack and I squeezed into a room at the Castle Star Hotel in Hugh Town on St. Mary's, the largest of the small islands.

Once we had unpacked, we took the kids for a swim in the hotel pool, believing it to be vital to keep busy, particularly when the news wasn't good. We wandered down the cobbled streets to St. Mary's Yacht Club where, on their only telephone, up-to-date information was being relayed from the Megastore.

By now the news was somewhat better. The crew had mended the leaking fuel tank, the weather was calmer, and they were averaging 40 knots. Feeling more relaxed, we decided to sail over to Tresco, the second largest of the islands. As we glided through the clear water, surrounded by romping seals and puffins, it was almost possible to forget the purpose of our visit. Tresco was lovely and we enjoyed exploring its gardens and white sandy beaches.

We returned to the hotel to hear that the Challenger was only 245 nautical miles away from its goal and was being refuelled for the last time. The wind was between force 3 and 5; the Challenger was averaging 45 knots. Even the waves had subsided a little. Dag Pyke reported by radio: "We've got a superb boat here. It has taken everything we've thrown at it, although without a wink of sleep, we are beginning to feel we have been at sea for far more than three days. We'll be glad to see our beds. Over."

Next came a call advising the team that Princess Michael would definitely be at the Hamble the following day for the noontime victory reception.

Excitement was building at the Club. The main room was packed with press. On the pier outside, tourists and locals gathered in groups, chatting happily. The Challenger crew's wives rushed back to their lodgings to pack and dress up for the hastily planned reception party. Afterwards, we were all going to fly back by helicopter to Eastleigh with Richard and his crew before attending the royal reception on the Hamble the next day.

As everyone was getting ready at the Club, the Flag Officer of the Royal Western at Plymouth was flown out to Bishop's Rock, where he would act as the official timekeeper. At the rate they were going, they should beat the record by at least two hours, passing the Rock at around 8pm.

Photographer Colin Taylor left at 4pm in a twin-engine airbus to get an aerial view of the finish. I was busy helping cut up hundreds of blue fabric streamers that would fly from every craft in the harbour. The mood of excitement and anticipation was infectious. Even the ex-Prime Minister, Harold Wilson, wandered out of his bungalow to see what all the commotion was about. It seemed ironic that a Labour politician should be present in the midst of such an unabashedly free market enterprise!

With the end in sight, it was time for Ted and me to go to the hotel and pack up to leave. We had almost finished when we heard someone run up the stairs and bang on our door. It was the hotel manager, looking anxious.

"They want you at the Club," he shouted. "It's urgent. There has been a May Day alert."

Ted and I looked at each other nervously. "Shall we bring our suitcases?" I asked.

"No, leave everything. Just come with me—quick."

White and shaking, we arrived at the Club. People were standing around outside, looking on in silence as the island's lifeboat roared away from the pier. We made our way through the crowds, past the cameramen and reporters who were, for once, standing by silently. One of the ground crew guided us into the small banquet hall. There we found the crew's wives looking pale and downcast. They had just seen an emergency announcement on the TV: "The Virgin Atlantic Challenger has sunk 138 nautical miles short of achieving its goal." After hitting a massive wave, the hull had split open and the crew had launched two rubber lifeboats.

We stood around in terrible silence. No one said much, as we knew the crew could all be drowned. It was a dark moment in my life, but I knew Ted and I had to pull ourselves together and look after the others. I felt like a mother to the other wives as I went around comforting them. One was sobbing quietly, another was hysterical and a third was pacing feverishly. The only one who seemed to take it in her stride was Chay Blyth's wife, Maureen. She had experienced it all before.

There was no more news. We tried to give them hope, suggesting that a helicopter or passing boat might have picked up the crew. After all, the Challenger had sunk not far off the coast. My only way to cope was to stay busy helping others and try to forget that our son was out there too.

About two hours passed, though it felt like 10, before we heard that two life rafts had been sighted from the air. We felt a pang of relief but then began to fear for Joan. She had probably seen the news bulletin on TV. I went outside to use the only phone available but it was surrounded by a swarm of reporters fighting to file their copy. Luckily a Virgin rep sneaked me out a back door to a nearby cottage where we were able to use another phone.

"Is Richard all right?" Joan asked nervously. It was desperately difficult to answer her. No one knew whether Richard and the crew were dead or alive. I could only reassure her with bland, rather evasive answers that I would know more shortly. I asked her to turn off the radio and TV. She must not listen to anyone except me, I told her. I said I would ring her back when I heard something definite.

Now news was arriving every minute. A helicopter had sighted the crew in their lifeboats. The nearest craft to them was Geetsbay, a banana boat heading for Jamaica, and it wasn't long before Richard and the crew were winched on board.

That evening, when they joined the passengers in the Geetsbay Captain's quarters for dinner, an elderly woman handed Richard a copy of that day's London *Evening Standard* with a photograph of Sam, his new baby, on the front page. What joy in the midst of such drama!

✈

Back at St. Mary's Yacht Club, a bus was arranged for the families to be taken to the airport, where the nine members of the crew had been flown in by helicopter. Tired and unshaven, they were waiting in a line for us in their dirty, sodden overalls whilst we were all smartly dressed in our finery, ready for the victory party we had been anticipating. The reunion with Richard was as emotional as anything I had ever experienced.

At midnight, we all boarded a helicopter to take us to Eastleigh. Someone had even managed to rustle up champagne and sandwiches. We all had our own stories to relate on the flight back. There was a touch of war spirit about the scene. We were like soldiers returning from the front line, trading grim stories above a din of the rotary blades, trying not to show too much emotion.

Utterly exhausted, we arrived at our hotel in Eastleigh. As I lay in bed, I wondered whether Richard would try again to capture the Blue Riband for Britain. Of course he would. Defeat is what inspires him to succeed.

The following day we were all refreshed, but seeing the headlines in the papers with the sight of the Challenger's bow poking up through the choppy Atlantic waters made me feel both sad and proud. It had been failure on the grandest scale: glorious, dangerous, and somehow very British—a brave underdog struggling against all odds, a spectacle guaranteed to touch the nation's heart.

For Richard, of course, it was only the beginning. Even as they were hauling him out of the water, he was saying, "Don't worry everyone, we'll be back to do it again." My heart skipped a beat when I heard those words because I knew he meant it.

The challenge was on. Ever since Richard was a child, he was inspired by adversity. When he played tennis, he liked to lose the first few games. Only then could he put his back into it and win the match.

Ted and I dreaded the next attempt. Did he really have to try this again? Why not leave it for someone else? But as his parents, we knew that wasn't Richard's style: a true adventurer never quits after only one try.

ATLANTIC CROSSING, REDUX

A year later, the family gathered at the Brooke Marine shipbuilding yard in Lowestoft to witness what we hoped would be the turning point in Richard's gruelling battle with the Atlantic. Friends, relatives and the press had converged from all parts of Britain on a rather bleak, windy May morning for the launch of the Virgin Atlantic Challenger II.

I arrived with Joan, Holly and little Sam. Ted came by helicopter with Richard, Clare, and my mother, now 88. It was an exciting day for all of us. What other businessmen invite their families, including their grannies, aunts and uncles, to join in their adventures?

✈

Most of the press coverage Richard receives is pretty favourable. This time, however, some journalists were beginning to wonder about his mental health. One article, in particular, by the *Daily Mail* columnist Ian Wooldridge stuck in my mind:

> Since the demise of hair shirts and religious flagellation, the sincerely rich have been at their wits' end to discover new ways to punish themselves. Richard doesn't think about it. He's looking forward to his annual penance on the Atlantic's most dangerous and uncomfortable crossing. "Last time," he says, like a man who has just paid his dues for success, "it took me a week to get the ringing noises out of my ears. I was beginning to think I had permanent brain damage."

Reading this, I tried hard not to dwell on the dangers of the Atlantic challenge. I couldn't afford to trigger my imagination. I just wanted to put my blinkers on. Ian Wooldridge had a point; Richard did have a mad streak in him, but never quite to the point of self-destruction. He would drive a car so fast that it seemed dangerous, but somehow always managed to keep it just under control. He knows how to push himself near the limit and get away with it. It's all about knowing where the edge is.

Take Challenger II, for example: everything on that craft had been carefully thought out. Richard and his staff had arranged for the very best crew, engineers and designers, which gave us the confidence that a successful crossing was possible.

It is rather like watching your child climbing a tree. As a parent, all you can do is to make sure that there are no rotten branches. If the child falls anyway, well, it's terribly bad luck, but the risk is essential for their development. The only problem with the

Challenger adventure was that in this case, I was not allowed to check for dead branches!

It was decided that the £1.5 million Virgin Atlantic Challenger II would follow the exact same route as the SS United States, which crossed from New York to Bishop Rock Lighthouse in 3 days, 10 hours and 40 minutes at an average speed of 35-59 knots.

"In order to have a chance at breaking the record, we will need to average 45 knots," Dag told us. "The route will include three refuelling points—the first off Halifax, Nova Scotia, and the next about 200 miles to the east of St John's, Newfoundland in what is called the Flemish Pass. The final refuelling will be a delicate operation in the mid-Atlantic from an offshore vessel."

Ted and I caught each other's eye. In times like these, Ted, Richard and I hardly talked to each other, but we were acutely conscious of each other's presence, perhaps sharing the odd wink. The reality of it all was fast dawning on me. Everyone around us was swilling champagne and nibbling on Beluga caviar. The mood was heady and light. I pushed my plate aside and tried to shut out the unpleasant thoughts racing through my mind.

After a few weather delays, Rick called from New York to say they were leaving the next morning at 2.30am New York time. "Love to all. See you at breakfast on Sunday."

✈

On Saturday, after a tense 24 hours monitoring the Challenger II's progress from the communications centre at the Virgin Megastore, Ted and I headed down to Plymouth, and then to the Scilly Isles to await the Challenger's return. It felt like déjà vu! When we arrived, helicopters and private planes were circling overhead, carrying journalists and cameramen representing media from throughout the world.

We went immediately to St. Mary's Yacht Club, where we heard the news that water in the Challenger II's fuel rank had brought the boat to a stop three times.

We listened anxiously as Rick called in. "May win it by an hour or lose it by an hour, maybe a minute. Can't push it too hard. Boat may break up." A moment later he continued, "Can the people of the Scilly please move their island so the finishing line can be a bit closer?"

The next morning we woke up to hear the screeching of the gulls and the 7 o'clock news about the Challenger II. The Irish Navy had carried out its third and last refuelling, a brilliantly quick operation that took 33 minutes to load 2,844 gallons of diesel instead of the hour they had anticipated. Richard said over the radio that this had been a great morale booster to the somewhat tired and battered crew who hadn't slept for three nights. They were also grateful for the thick, nourishing soup the Irish crew served them.

Next came word that the crew was optimistic. Challenger II was cresting six-foot waves, coping well under the strain, and the crew was getting the 10-odd minutes of sleep, and singing and dancing to keep awake. Their morale was high and though they were very tired, they kept up 42 knots.

At 5.30pm, the Club was buzzing with excitement. It really looked like they'd make it this time. ETA was 7.30pm, and every available vessel—canoes, rowing boats, yachts, speedboats and Sicilian Pilot Rigs—was angling to get the first glimpse of the Challenger II passing the Bishop Rock Lighthouse.

Small planes and helicopters were still arriving, anxious to be there for the finish. The quayside was now nearly full to capacity and every available Scillian was helping in some way, preparing for the reception, putting up the bunting or collecting the crew's wives and families from hotels and cottages.

It had started to rain but that did not dampen anyone's spirits, least of all ours, as we were swept off to sail beyond the Bishop Rock Lighthouse in the launch owned by Robert Dorrien-Smith, the proprietor of the island of Tresco. We saw three specks of light on the horizon that turned out to be the headlights of three approaching helicopters. We then spotted two white plumes of spray and finally saw the Challenger itself advancing towards us at 50 knots.

We headed back toward the Lighthouse with boat sirens and hooters sounding at full blast all around us. Soon the timekeeper, who was stationed at the lighthouse, announced over a loudspeaker that the five-man Challenger II crew had crossed over the finishing line in three days, eight hours and 31 minutes, knocking 129 minutes off the record set by the 53,000-ton American liner. What an achievement for the crew of this 72-foot speedboat!

Ted and I were ecstatic as we joined the jubilant crowd heading back to the Club, all staying as close as possible to the Challenger II, with the Scilly lifeboat hovering close by.

The crowd shouted and cheered as the boat finally stopped near the quay with the very relieved but tired crew waving from the deck. When a bottle of champagne was handed to Richard, no sooner had he managed to pop the cork than Chay Blyth, Steve Ridgeway, Dag Pyke and Peter Macann threw him overboard, much to the delight of the onlookers. There were many more cheers as Chay then threw an inflated rubber mermaid to Rick's aid!

We all moved to the quayside where Prince Michael and the local mayor greeted Rick and the crew. There were speeches all round and more cheers as the Prince handed them a model of Bishop Rock Lighthouse encased in an old lighthouse bulb, a memento made by a member of the lighthouse staff on behalf of the people of the Scilly Isles. Finally the party moved to the Club before the exuberant crowd and exhausted crew made their way home to bed.

✈

On Monday morning we awoke to the sound of small planes and helicopters leaving the island and walked down to the quayside to see the Challenger II in the daylight. The little quay was almost sinking under the weight of the crowds clamouring for Rick's autograph. Overhead, the Air Sea Rescue helicopter flew low over Challenger II with a "Well done" banner streaming behind it. Well done indeed; it was the very same helicopter that had winched them to safety after the Challenger sank the year before!

Two days later, the Challenger II was brought up the Thames to celebrate its victory with Londoners. We were invited on board Rick's pleasure steamer, The New Elizabethan, and along with the press and the crew's wives and friends, we steamed up to the Tower of London, arriving just in time to see the Tower Bridge slowly open in salute. The Challenger II roared past at 50 knots followed by a burst of fireworks and cheers from the crowds on both sides of the river. Finally it sped past a fire tender opposite us that joined in this spectacular welcome by shooting jets of water hundreds of feet in the air.

She finally stopped at Tower Pier where Princess Michael of Kent was waiting to greet her and congratulate Rick and the crew. Somehow we were unaware that Prime Minister Thatcher was also on board our boat, waiting to be whisked down the Thames on Challenger II to the reception.

Whether the Americans would actually give up the Hales Trophy seemed of little consequence to me. Rick had now thrown down the gauntlet for other contenders. I had no doubt that he would be happy to pass the trophy on to whichever country beat his crew's record. I just hoped we wouldn't need to wait another 34 years to get it back.

As Rick's mother, I was very glad he got this particular obsession out of his system. And though my message to him then was, "Well done, Rick; thanks for those exciting few days," I wouldn't wish the stress of such an event on any other mother!

CHAPTER 8

I N MAY 1987, TED AND I prepared to share vicariously in yet another adventure when we accepted an invitation to attend a press conference at the Explorers Club in Piccadilly. Oh, whatever next? I thought. The purpose of the event had been kept secret from us and from the media too. When we arrived, we found the room packed with journalists and cameramen. The curtain parted to reveal Richard and famed pilot and balloonist Per Lindstrand, both dressed in flight suits and standing against a backdrop of "Project Yankee—The Transatlantic Balloon Challenge of 1987."

I held my breath as they announced their intention to cross the Atlantic in a hot air balloon. Ben Abruzzo, Maxie Anderson and Larry Newman had successfully crossed the Atlantic in their conventional helium balloon, the Double Eagle II, in 1978. But no one had ever managed to make the crossing in a hot air balloon, which would explain Richard's single-minded objective to do just that.

The first manned flight in a hot air balloon was made in France in 1783 when Jacques-Étienne Montgolfier managed a short flight in a linen balloon fitted with burners filled with straw, surely astonishing onlookers by rising to 6,000 feet. And two years later, the world's first airmail delivery letter was carried across the English Channel in a helium balloon.

Maxie Anderson was quoted as saying that it would be impossible to cross the Atlantic in a hot air balloon, as the craft could carry only enough fuel for a few hours' flying time. These words were about to be challenged!

The clubroom, packed to capacity with media, fell silent as Per explained that the balloon had been made at his factory, Thunder & Colt, in Oswestry. He said it was the largest balloon ever built, bigger than a jumbo jet; it would fill three quarters of Wembley Football Stadium and at 195 feet, and it was taller than Nelson's column. At 170 feet wide when fully inflated (over double the length of a tennis court), it was capable of carrying 14 tons.

Per went on to say that the balloon, which would be called Virgin Flyer, would have just one life. It would survive one inflation, one launch, and one landing and would never fly again. The conference ended with much excitement and applause. Champagne was served to toast this daring new challenge, but Ted and I just looked at one another, dumbfounded. Nonetheless we dutifully went home to prepare to fly from London to Maine to observe this bold adventure.

✈

When we arrived in Boston with Richard on 19 June, the customs officer asked, "Business or pleasure?" For once Richard was lost for an answer. Just what was the true nature of this exploit?

We went on to Maine, where we would be staying at the Sugarloaf Mountain Hotel in Kingfield, a small ski resort nestled in the deep wilderness of the state's Western Mountains. Cars, helicopters, and planes brought in press and TV crews from all over the world. Takeoff was scheduled in 48 hours.

Two rooms had been allocated in the hotel for operations and media. Not getting any more accustomed to being witness to our son's dangerous endeavours, Ted and I were excited but anxious. Could Richard really be leaving America for England in a small capsule with nothing but the wind to take him across the Atlantic?

CHAPTER 8

Meanwhile, up the coast in St. John's, Newfoundland, a rival balloonist, Don Cameron, was also preparing to cross the Atlantic. As a competitive tension mounted between the two adventurers, Richard summed up the scenario perfectly: "We are not in a race; we are just two gentlemen doing our own thing." (Don Cameron never did take off.)

On 20 June the weather was hot, with not a breath of wind. I went to have a look at the capsule being worked on by ground technicians, a spectacle resembling a scene from a science fiction movie. Screws and bolts were everywhere. It seemed impossible that this odd-looking capsule, measuring 7 feet 10 inches in diameter, with an overall height of 8 feet 1 inch, would be ready to fly the next day.

Not wanting to disturb the workers, I ambled across the road to find the balloon, all alone and waiting patiently to come to life, the 12 miles of material stowed in the back of a small freight truck.

My feelings fluctuated between fear and excitement, but try as I might, I found it impossible to relax. I strolled down to the village green, nestled beneath trees in the shadow of the Bigelow Mountains. Could this peaceful green possibly be big enough to give birth to this great balloon?

By the next morning bad weather was closing in. Bob Rice, chief meteorologist, clearly feeling the burden of holding both men's lives in his hands, announced, "Project temporarily cancelled till Thursday." Oh, the relief!

✈

With time to fill, Ted, Richard and I decided to join five other brave souls to try white-water rafting for the first time. We drove through the magnificent countryside, occasionally passing an inquisitive moose grazing in the greenery alongside the road. At last we arrived at The Forks and met our rafting guide Joe, who would make all the decisions on our river journey.

Joe gave us each a paddle and explained that it was the most important instrument in the sport. We then learnt the commands, the most critical being "Back paddle!"—when he yelled that, we knew we'd better do it or else! Our brief lesson over, we carried our raft down the steep embankment to the Kennebec River.

Before the eight of us climbed aboard, we had to decide whether to sit in the bow or the stern of the craft. In the bow you can feel more impact of each peak as you ride it; towards the stern you get a rocking motion and bumps, similar to being in a car on a bumpy road. I chose the bow. By now I was silently gripped with intense fear, but if Richard could cross the Atlantic in a balloon, surely I should be brave enough to shoot the rapids!

Rafting through the majestic falls, we experienced exhilaration beyond our wildest dreams. The guide bellowed: "Pull right! All ahead! Hold on!" and the ubiquitous "Back paddle!"

Our three rubber boats swept down through the 12-mile-long Kennebec River Gorge, which gushed more than 40,000 gallons of clear, clean, drinkable water per second. The first four-mile drop was approximately 100 feet per mile. Once we started, there was no stopping as we raced through the wilderness, ducking and bobbing over giant waves. Finally, the inevitable happened and into the drink went Richard, on purpose or by mistake I wasn't sure! One by one the crew followed overboard and to my horror, I thought I was alone until I looked back with relief to see that our rafting guide was still aboard.

A somewhat wet and bedraggled little party arrived back at the hotel to hear that the weather was further deteriorating, the mountains now covered in clouds. Relief once more!

At this news, Richard and a few others decided to return to England, leaving Ted and me to enjoy the many pleasures of Maine. This respite helped us to forget the real reason we were there and we revelled in the wonderful hospitality of the local people, challenging them in baseball and joining them to fish for trout. At the local sports centre, we enjoyed many pleasant hours of tennis, golf and swimming. But a short week later, we were brought back to reality when Bob Rice, weather guru, summoned Richard back, as it seemed that the all-important good weather window was imminent.

By Wednesday 1 July, the Sugarloaf Hotel was abuzz as cars, helicopters, jets and satellite trucks brought media, tourists and well-wishers from around the world. This sleepy ski resort was bursting with activity in anticipation of the balloon launch, though the weather for the moment was still wet and windy.

At the final press conference in the hotel ballroom, about 300 press representatives strained to get the last details. I crept into the back so I could hear Per and Richard speak to the crowd of reporters and calmly answer their questions.

"Bob Rice has now given us the all-clear for take-off tomorrow at dawn," Per announced. "There is a good strong east-to-west jet stream. We will be climbing at a rate of 100 feet per minute till we reach our cruising height of 30,000 feet, which should happen at midday. There will be no second chance." By now my heart was thumping and I could feel my anxiety rising by the minute.

Answering a query about the amount of fuel needed, Per reiterated the vital importance of the sun, which for 18 hours a day would provide supplemental fuel. The main capsule, also known as the envelope, surrounded by another transparent envelope, would create a greenhouse effect, warming the balloon and providing most of the fuel needed for the flight.

A reporter asked why Richard was undertaking the flight. "To have the chance in one's lifetime to hold one world record is challenging enough; to have the chance of creating a new one makes me feel very fortunate," he said. "The project is a fascinating combination of adventure in its truest sense, in creative design and engineering skills, yet it remains true to the principles of the very first flight that man ever made. This is a real challenge, to go one step further than anyone has ever gone before."

✈

Richard's words were inspiring but they did little to alleviate my fear and dread of something going wrong. After the press conference, the media made a mad dash to grab the few telephones available to get their stories to their editors. Once more Ted and I were left speechless, filled with anxiety, fear and admiration. How we wished Richard wasn't the one taking this risk! And yet my feelings were mixed, as I too loved adventure and would join him if I could!

The following day I kept busy; it was the only way I could put the ordeal ahead out of my mind. I spent the day helping to answer the telephones in the operations room. All 12 phones flashed red lights nonstop and telex machines worked overtime, as did the coffee machines.

Richard was in and out, organising permits to land both east and west of Europe; because of the jet stream, Finland and Russia appeared to be possible landing areas. One glorious wink across the room from Richard kept me going on an adrenaline high. I dashed down to the nearest chemist to buy Per and Richard seasick pills and a lucky moose mascot. The weather was getting calmer whilst Ted's and my nerves were getting more ragged!

✈

At last the launch approached. The massive balloon was removed from the freight container and transported down to the launch site. By 10.30pm, ground crews began the delicate task of inflating the balloon, with two hours of cold air followed by several hours of hot air. About 40 technicians ringed the canopy that had been unfolded on the grassy verge cordoned off by security.

During the inflation process the envelope was at its most vulnerable, as the partially inflated double-skinned balloon would begin to rise off the ground and have to be restrained. Like a vast spinnaker it would catch every puff of breeze. If the balloon snagged on something and tore, the months of planning would be wasted.

Bob Rice had chosen this launch site because of the natural bowl configuration at the foot of the mountains, a perfect location where the cold night air settled and offered hours of virtually windless conditions.

By midnight I'd left my telephone post to hasten down to the launch site to see the hot air being pumped into the balloon, now a quarter full and floodlit, with its capsule lying on its side. Police, fire engines, firefighters, ambulances and medical crews were in attendance. Hundreds of spectators took the gondola to the peak of Sugar Loaf Mountain to spend the evening eating bagels and drinking mimosa tea. I could not think about relaxing; instead I was overwhelmed with what was becoming a familiar feeling—my emotions were being pulled in all directions.

By 2.30am the sky was clear, the weather utterly calm and quite cold for a summer night. This was important because hot air balloons fly better in the cold due to the density of the atmosphere. The cold would make the Virgin Atlantic Flyer easier to handle at the launch. Balloon and capsule were now upright, raring to go, save for the sandbags holding her tethers down, a breathtaking sight.

This huge silver-topped, black-sheathed envelope, never before tested, was magnificent but frightening too.

In a silent daze I walked round and round the green, wanting to be left alone but constantly being approached by the press. "What are your thoughts?" they would ask. It was an impossible question to answer.

At 3.00am, all eyes turned to see the police escorting Per and Richard, dressed in flight suits, carrying their helmets and kid gloves. Turning the corner, they stopped to behold a magnificent sight; floodlights beamed onto the capsule and the balloon glimmered majestically in the moonlight. She was ready to go. Conditions were perfect.

I turned to Ted, both of us very emotional, realising that there was no turning back. Then, with Per's wife, we were taken to have a last word with the pilots in the capsule. I can hardly remember what Ted and I said to Richard but we stayed positive—there was no use in showing him how terrified we were.

By now the crowds were silent, listening to the screeching of the four compressors, which burned fiercely to keep the balloon inflated.

Finally, at 3.40am, it was time for the countdown: ten, nine, eight, seven, six....The ground crew released her tethers, leaving only sandbags attached. The Virgin Flyer slowly rose off her haunches, flames raging from the four burners. It rose just a foot or two into the air as the crowd cheered and then WHAM! Two of the dozen tanks of liquid propane fuel strapped to the balloon's side tore free from the capsule and crashed to the ground. A gasp from the crowd! An explosion seemed inevitable so the firefighters moved closer to the balloon and security personnel quickly evacuated the area.

No explosion came, though, and the huge balloon carried on gracefully, silently continuing its lift. We were relieved that no one had been hurt when the fuel tanks dropped, but how serious was the loss of fuel to the crew?

The pink glow of sunrise now appeared behind the Bigelow Mountains as this magnificent balloon sailed softly up, up and away, floating free to ride the westerly winds high above Sugarloaf Mountain. As it rose, the balloon cast a huge shadow over the launch pad. It became smaller and smaller until it disappeared. Yes, it was on its way.

✈

We uttered a few prayers to the winds, asking them to carry the balloon and its crew safely across the ocean. But there was no time to linger. We were bundled into a car to return to the hotel to pack. The race was on; the balloon was travelling at 117 miles per hour, much faster than expected. In order for us to arrive in time for the landing, we would have to catch the next Virgin 747 to England.

By 8.45am the balloon was reported over Halifax, Nova Scotia, having covered 590 miles in six hours. Back in the States, though, weather was closing in again. Newark Airport was closed, so we had to land in Augusta and consider alternative ways of beating the balloon back home. Eventually the weather lifted and we were able to make it to Newark just in time to catch our flight to Gatwick.

Hurrying across the Atlantic in the Virgin jet, Virgin Scarlet Lady, was nerve-wracking but thrilling too. At 6.15pm our captain announced that the balloon was almost halfway across the Atlantic with only 35 hours to go. It had been flying at 27,000 feet for the last six hours, averaging 92 knots per hour, and appeared to be headed for Scotland.

All the passengers were peering through the portholes when a flight attendant touched my shoulder. The captain had invited Ted and me into the cockpit to see something extraordinary: our jet was sandwiched between Richard's balloon, flying at 27,000 feet, and the Speedbird Concorde above, flying at 55,000 feet.

Having gained special permission from traffic control, we dropped 4,000 feet in order to salute the balloon. It truly seemed like a dream, seeing this silvery bubble bouncing above the woolly white clouds. Now able to talk directly and clearly over the radio to Richard, I could only say, "Faster, Richard. We'll race you."

He answered very clearly, "I'm doing my best, Mum" and then asked us to thank the captain and crew for flying over him. We hoped it might be a comfort for them to know that we were close by and in contact. Then Captain Hayward took over the microphone to say he was dropping to 28,000 feet to circle the Flyer and do a figure eight so all the passengers on either side of the plane could see the balloon! At the rate they were going, it would be in England in five or six hours' time, and was expected to land somewhere in the North.

We touched down at 2.45pm and went directly to the busy Gatwick Heliport waiting room. Due to the unexpected speed of the balloon, there had been little time for the project team to organise transportation to the landing location for the ground recovery crew, media and other spectators. After receiving updates on wind directions and possible destinations for the balloon landing, Ted and I and Per's wife boarded a helicopter and dropped down at the Battersea Heliport where we quickly picked up Lindy before speeding to Carlisle to refuel. Meanwhile, the balloon was heading off Northern Ireland, so we were able to cut a corner en route to where we expected it to land. But things would not go as planned!

✈

As the hours passed, I wrote in my diary:

18.45pm: I heard that Richard and Per had touched the sea, the North Channel between Scotland and Ireland, but were now heading for Northern Ireland. It all sounded a bit odd! How could they have touched the sea and still be flying? Luckily I had Penni Pike's phone number and hastily phoned her, saying no one seemed to know where to go—she told us to head for the North of Ireland, though the press had all gone to Scotland. I said thanks and off we flew!

We could see them on our radar screen off the Mull of Kintyre and were all very excited as we chopped past Ailsa Craig and over the lowlands of Scotland. But an hour and a half later we heard over the radio that the crew had landed in the sea. Richard had been picked up by a boat, alive but hurt; no news yet about Per.

It was now raining. We sat in nervous silence, all peering fearfully into the mysterious ocean.

19.10pm: We were all alone with our own quiet thoughts, save for the beat of the helicopter blades. We were instructed to keep the radio beacon off, as it was only for emergency calls.

19.11pm: Now Per was officially reported missing at sea and all aircraft in the vicinity on the alert were asked to look out for him. Per's wife was magnificent, no hysterics, but her face slowly drained of colour.

19.12pm: Heard Per had been sighted swimming for shore. Later we learned that Per was in the water below us with no life raft, swimming for two and a half hours against heavy currents.

19.20pm: Just heard Per had been picked up some four miles off Rathlin Island by a Sea King Helicopter. Now we had full view of the balloon that was lying in the water with the capsule still attached. Just what could have happened?

19.30pm: A speedboat below and only two other rescue helicopters above—time for thought. Our son hurt? But he's alive!

19.45pm: Watched Richard being winched up in one of the rescue helicopters. Ted and I felt hopeful—surely his injuries couldn't be too bad? In convoy we followed them to Kilmarnoc Hospital. We were surprised that out of all the people who came over from America and set off from Gatwick, we were the only ones who arrived in time to see the end of the balloon crossing.

✈

Finally the three helicopters touched down at Kilmarnoc, Ayrshire. Richard and Per descended, white and shaken, drenched through and wrapped in blankets, amidst a cheering multitude that seemed to appear from nowhere. Police struggled to make a path to the waiting ambulance. Lindy fought the crowds back, helping to make way for her injured brother.

Richard and Per were taken to two private rooms for medical checks while press, friends and media waited outside for news of their conditions. Not long afterward, they both appeared in the waiting room of the small cottage hospital to speak to the press.

Could it have been only two days ago that we attended a similar press conference in America at the start of this ordeal?

Ted and I were at the back of the room, listening to Per and Richard describe their harrowing experience, still in shock but overcome with relief that they had survived.

At the end of the press briefing, the matron of the small cottage hospital appeared with a telegram from 10 Downing Street, which she read aloud:

I was sorry to hear about the dramatic end to your adventure, though relieved to know that neither of you is seriously hurt. Your crossing has been a brave and magnificent achievement. I send you every good wish for a speedy recovery.

Margaret Thatcher, Prime Minister

I was happy that Richard was making his country proud. Yet as his mother, I was also hoping that his words to *The Morning Sun* before leaving Maine on 2 July were true. When asked about future plans, he said he hoped to try and start being a more sensible individual.

Did or didn't I hope this would happen? Yes, Richard, leave it now to someone else. Enough's enough!

✈

Back at home, we enjoyed life at Cakeham and Ted was happy with my decision to move there. We'd beautifully organised the cellar with shelves full of his books. We'd also organised all his tools, so he could find them easily, unlike at Tanyards where they were always in a jumble.

I now understood why the family thought we were mad to move to a bigger house with an even bigger garden to care for. Perhaps we were but we loved the place. Here we would continue the tradition of giving an annual party for the Virgin staff that worked in London. How they all loved a day in the country! I'd lay on a steel band, lots of beer, booze and a sumptuous lunch. They'd play croquet, tennis, rounders in the field or just lie on the lawn and enjoy being in the countryside.

✈

But adventure would soon lure us from settling too comfortably into country life and before we knew it, Ted and I and my sister Clare were off to Japan to witness Richard's next challenge: flying a balloon over the Pacific, a mere 6,200 miles. My only thought was, "Here we go again!"

We flew to Japan and drove to the small town of Miyakomojo, where the locals had arranged an ancient Shinto ceremony in a huge baseball stadium where the launch was to take place. During the early evening ceremony, monks dressed in white robes, black clogs and exotic hats proceeded slowly to an altar that had been laid out next to the balloon capsule. They clapped their hands twice to summon the gods for their attention before they blessed the capsule itself. Then they came forward one by one, shaking flower petals over the capsule, wishing it a safe passage. Needless to say, they weren't the only ones.

The next morning, we had a surprise in store, as Clare, Ted, Richard and I were swept up to the mountains by two enterprising journalists from the *Daily Telegraph* and *The Independent* who were looking for exclusives with Richard. They had found one of the oldest, most secluded natural spring baths in the area. The early morning sun and a haze of sulphur seeped through the low clouds as we clambered up the narrow path with boulders and waterfalls on either side.

We came upon two natural rock pools in a cave and although the air was very cold, the water was steaming hot. This we discovered to our joy after we had all stripped off, with Clare and I in one pool and the men in the other. But after much giggling from the pools and bamboo huts, the boys invited us to join them, so clutching our towels tightly, we ran through the sulphur steam and plunged into their pool!

The two journalists floated a beautiful tray over to us, laid out perfectly with a small flask of sake and four little cups. What a heavenly place to drink sake; the gods must surely have heard our laughter! That's what I call journalism with a difference. They must have had made a fortune out of that photograph!

Enough hilarity though, for Richard had to return for a parachute rehearsal. On our way down the mountain we stopped to climb a small hill that led to another bubbling sulphur spring. There we met three aerobic teachers dancing in the mist. The scene was enchanting and intoxicating and they invited us all to dance together amidst the sulphur fog. It was a welcome distraction for us all.

We soon returned to reality and Richard went on ahead of us. I tried not to think of the ordeal to come, the very reason we were there enjoying a clear morning sky as the dawn's pink mist slowly evaporated. Now I felt anxious. The mechanisms in the 10-ton capsule, the biggest ever built, were much more complicated than the last one. Richard and Per would have to travel more than double the distance of the transatlantic crossing, taking approximately 100 hours to reach the west coast of America.

✈

Back at our hotel, we heard the balloon project was on yellow/red alert and they expected a green light the next day. Oh, what emotions! I didn't know if I should laugh or cry.

I was fine until Richard joked with me, "Now, Mum, remember should I come to grief, you will have to carry on the family tradition and take my place as the balloonist. Being so much smaller, you should find the capsule more comfortable than I will!" Before leaving us, he tossed off one last crack: "Oh, by the way, Mum, a journalist from ITN has brought my obituary with her. You might care to check it." I felt sick.

"Be off, Richard! I'll see you later!" was all I could manage, fighting back tears.

✈

By the following day there was an active buzz at the site, with mechanics and electricians, dressed in red overalls, climbing like ants all over the capsule, adding the finishing touches to this truly wondrous work of art. The local children were picking up any rubbish lying around. Japanese gardeners were busily planting trees on the circumference whilst barriers and fences were being erected. Electricians, wires and television trucks were everywhere.

That evening we joined our Japanese hosts and other hotel guests in a traditional washing ceremony. The ladies were segregated—kimonos abandoned—for a plunge in the indoor hot spring bath, followed by a dip in the icy cold tub and then a stroll outside in the cold air before plunging into the steaming hot rock pool. There we wallowed, looking up to the stars until we could take the heat no longer and went back indoors for a shower and sauna.

But our relaxation didn't last long. In the next two days, the high winds made it impossible for the balloon to take off and then, incredibly, the first frost in the area in 15 years damaged it, creating tears in the outer foil, making it impossible to fly at all.

Richard and Per told the disappointed crowds, now numbering near 15,000, not to worry; they promised they would return again the following year and bring a spare balloon!

✈

Life has a way of balancing itself out. The Pacific crossing was postponed, but we would all soon gather at Necker for the happiest of occasions: Richard's marriage to Joan on December 20, 1989. The marriage itself was eight-year-old Holly's idea and we were all thrilled. This would be a wedding attended only by relatives, close friends and key employees of the various Virgin groups. My mother, 91, was flown in by helicopter to join her very excited great grandchildren. Could there be a more romantic setting than Necker to get married? Though it was once wild and uninhabited, it was now on its way to becoming a luxury resort.

It was a perfect day. The entire house was garlanded with exotic flowers and plants. Holly and Sam were dressed in cream satin suits whilst Joan arrived on her brother's arm, also dressed in cream satin and a full tulle veil. A most memorable event was the arrival of her groom, also dressed in a cream-coloured suit, who made his dramatic entrance dangling from a helicopter!

After the registrar pronounced Richard and Joan man and wife, we enjoyed champagne, speeches, superb food and dancing to a steel band. This surely was a wedding to be remembered!

CHAPTER 9

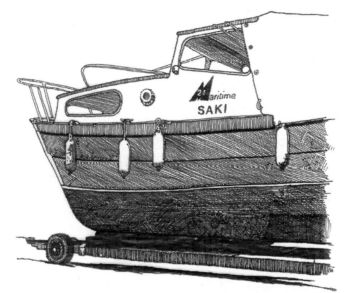

WHILST RICHARD WAS BUSY TRAIPSING the globe and making headlines with his adventures, Vanessa and Lindy were engaged in exciting challenges of their own. Vanessa was still running her successful picture gallery in Portobello Road, where she proved to have a keen eye for promising contemporary artists including the South African William Kentridge, whom she had backed early in his career. This was a relationship she was not to regret!

Lindy, meanwhile, was busy raising three boys and she and Robin, having married on Necker in 1985, hoped they might complete the family with a girl. What a splendid idea! However, on 24 February 1986, Lindy gave birth to not one but two more boys, twins Milo and Ludo. The following year, Vanessa and Robert were also thrilled to welcome their first son, christened Noah. Could it be that one day, these boys too would cause their parents the crazy mix of worry and pride their Uncle Richard had created for us? Only time would tell! For Ted and me, it was pure happiness to count that we now had eight grandchildren!

✈

Back home in England, I decided that I wanted to spend more time helping others, but who and how? I had recently heard about babies in Romania, abandoned by their impoverished mothers at birth, who were taken to overcrowded orphanages to live. There they were injected with vitamins, only to later discover that, in some cases, the unsterilized needles had infected some of them with the AIDS virus.

Money was needed urgently and I wanted to help if I could. So I thought, why not organise a sporting tennis tournament at our very own Cakeham Manor to raise funds to help the orphans? I called a meeting with four friends who said they would each find 32 tennis players and organise their own tournament, producing finalists for the semi-finals and finals to be played at Cakeham on Easter Sunday. Meanwhile I would invite my London coach Dave Gab and my friend, the sportswriter April Todd, to come to Cakeham to help me.

So on a somewhat cold and windy afternoon in April, we made £890 cash for the Romanian orphans and the event was a huge success. We gave away prizes such as the Bjorn Borg Award for the best dressed player, the Chris Evert Award for the best mannered, the Jennifer Capriati Award for the best young player and the John McEnroe Award for the worst behaved!

Tea was followed by drinks in in the old chapel in the bottom of Cakeham's watchtower. The kids went on a treasure hunt in the garden to find Easter eggs we had hidden there. That night, a young friend of the family's rang up to say she had given up alcohol for Lent and wanted to give the £110 she had saved to the Orphans Fund. We now had a grand total of £1,000 to give to the Romanian AIDS organisation. A satisfying Easter indeed!

✈

Next up was a weeklong trip to the River Test in Scotland with our old friends, our neighbours at Tanyards, where Ted and I would learn the rudiments of fly fishing. And guess what? I caught two long brown trout! What more could one wish for that to go fishing on a hot May day, with swans alighting nearby and ducks dotting the river banks, quite unaware of our hooks, which landed more often than not in the trees! The cuckoo was in full throttle, along with the wood pigeons and the odd moorhen, whilst the cows grazed peacefully behind us.

How quickly those seven days went by! And when we returned to Cakeham, there was great excitement on our very own pond. The Caroline duck walked proudly before us, followed by three fluffy babies. The population on the pond now consisted of seven charming residents: the Caroline duck and her babies, our original clipped wing Landy and one wild Mandarin.

Ted and I felt completely at home at Cakeham and made many improvements to the place in the next few years. Most important, we installed two new windows in our study and in the bedroom above so we could feast our eyes on the sea, Nabs Tower and the Isle of Wight. On summer evenings, we would get on our mountain bikes, our saddlebags filled with gin, whiskey and ice. With our faithful golden retriever Bella at our side, we'd pedal to East Head where we'd settle down in the sand dunes to watch the sun go down whilst the yachtsmen slowly sailed back up to their moorings.

✈

In August of 1990 we returned to Menorca, dividing the family up between our villa, Humble Pie, and Robin and Lindy's house, Venezia. We were now up to nine grandchildren, the youngest being Vanessa's little Florence, who was an easy guest. Not yet walking, she just sat and smiled at everything, gurgling with delight. Next in age was Noah, three, who could already swim the length of our pool. He would follow along bravely, copying many of the antics of the older children, from leaping off walls to sliding down an improvised bench seat that had been turned into a catapult seesaw.

We had one sticky drinks party; it was an uphill struggle until Noah came shooting past everyone on his three-wheeler, shouting, "Chips finished, party's over." That sure got them going!

✈

To live by the sea and not own a boat seemed a shame, so off I went to the London Boat Show to see if I could find something we could afford that the family would enjoy. Ignoring all the fibreglass fishing boats, I spied two Devon boat builders showing off a wooden boat and asked them about it. Yes, they made boats to order, they said, so down went my name! Each month, they promised to send me a Polaroid photo of their progress. In the months ahead, when each photo arrived, I placed it on the mantelpiece and the family got more and more excited about seeing the boat take shape.

At the end of September, the boat builders, Bob and Ben, called to say the boat was finished and they were bringing her up from Devon the next day. Hence I quickly planned another great christening for the latest baby in the family, the boat that I first named Sake after my favourite drink in Japan. Realizing that the name would look like the word "sake" and be pronounced that way, I changed the spelling of the name to Saki and painted those letters on the boat.

The christening took place at Birdham Pool, a marina near Cakeham. I asked thirty friends and family to be there at 11am. Ted and I were up early to prepare a picnic luncheon. It was a thrill to see little Saki still on her trailer, waiting for the launch.

Our friends and family arrived to watch her being lowered into the water. We doused her bow with champagne and Coca-Cola and held our glasses high in the air, toasting our future sailing adventures. Then Ted and I and a few of our guests climbed into the boat and left the harbour amidst shouts and hoots from the crowd. All was fine until we took a wrong turn and ended up back in Birdham Pool instead of out to sea! Never mind, the memory of this lovely boat will live on, as she was the inspiration for a book I wrote for my grandchildren—*Sarky Puddleboat*—about a magic boat that took them on grand adventures.

✈

Just a month later we received the news that made me grind my teeth ever so gently. Rick was back on his plan to fly from Japan to America once more in the largest balloon ever, hoping to catch the jet stream. I was fearful that, at age 40, he had been on enough dangerous missions, though I knew giving them up would be out of character.

We left Gatwick with fewer press than had joined us for the last attempt a year earlier, and there wasn't quite as much excitement. In fact, there was an air of quiet apprehension among us all.

CHAPTER 9

Arriving in Tokyo, we discovered that a typhoon was heading for southern Japan. Was that not the very area where Rick and Per planned to launch their balloon? We also heard that when the meteorological conditions were at their optimum for take-off at the launch site in Miyakonojo, the jet stream should be fast enough to carry the balloon up to 200 miles per hour, which would allow Richard and Per to make the crossing in less than 100 hours.

But the weather would not cooperate. The envelope was designed to minimise heat loss by capturing as much solar heat as possible during the day. During the night, the balloon would rely solely on its propane burners for lift.

Upon arrival at Miyakonojo Airport, we were greeted by the mayor and escorted to the Town Hall where school children greeted us. It was a wonderful reception, as children presented each of us with a rose followed by a goodbye wave with their homemade Union Jacks fluttering in their small hands.

Unfortunately, the transpacific balloon crossing would be postponed one more time, for about two months, so home we went to enjoy a family Christmas and usher in the New Year!

The Debutante!

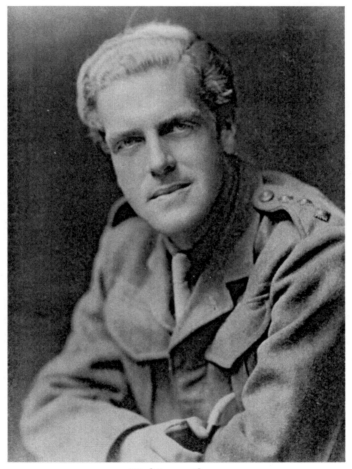

Ted in uniform

Mum and Dad

With brother Michael

Dancers escaping war worries, 1943

An aspiring actress

In my dancing days

After my Cochran's audition

Signalling at the end
of Yarmouth Pier, 1944

Flag-wagging!

In my ENSA uniform, 1945

On my wedding day, 1949

The Huntley-Flindts and Bransons at my wedding

Our first home, Easteds, Shamley Green

Early days

The Pram, 1954

With Ted, Eve, Richard and Lindy, circa 1957

Playing with seal pup

Putting up my feet!

Family moment, 1959

Always thirsty!

Ted launching the dinghy

Our house,
Humble Pie,
in Menorca

With the children on holiday

Margarita, our first wooden boat

Learning to type

Our second home, Tanyard Farm, Shamley Green

Lindy, Richard, and Vanessa in Scotland

Vanessa, Richard, and Lindy enjoying a toast

*Richard giving
his Granny a
helpful lift*

*With Mum
and Richard
on Virgin
Atlantic's
inaugural
flight from
London to
New York*

Holly and her dad

With little Holly

Sam and Holly

With grandson Jack
at Richard and Joan's
wedding, 1989

Discovering Necker

With Kevin Costner, Richard, Sir Roger
and Lady Moore in Monte Carlo

At the inaugural of
Virgin Vintage Airways

Biggles Branson!

Loyal secretary Penni Pike

Ted and Joan in Monte Carlo

Whatever next? A trans-Atlantic balloon challenge, of course!

Ted enjoys an inaugural event

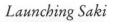
Launching Saki

At the book party for Sarky Puddleduck *with granddaughter Holly and editor pal*

Throw that one back!

With one of my Cashmere babies in the Atlas Mountains, Morocco

Girls in Morocco learn patchwork in an Eve Branson Foundation program

Girls learning to spin

Ludo, Milo, and Otto kitesurfing

Robin Brockway windsurfing with the ferry

*Cakeham
Manor, our
beautiful
family home*

*Cakeham Manor
in winter*

*Cakeham Pond
in winter*

With Ted and Richard

*With my editor
pal Holly Peppe*

Family photo on Necker Island

Daughter Lindy

Lindy and the boys

Vanessa and family

Daughter Vanessa

Holly and Freddie's joyous wedding on Necker, 2011

CHAPTER 10

AFTER A FALSE START THE previous November, we returned to Miyakonojo in January 1991 when the jet stream was perfect for Per and Richard to try to cross the Pacific in their hot air balloon—6,700 miles! They had set a new standard for long distance hot air ballooning with their Atlantic crossing, when they flew fast and high in the jet stream, buoyed by the sun. Now that the weather was cooperating, another record could be in store.

Ted and I planned to chase after the balloon, relying on reports from the flight control base in Los Angeles where all the weather information would be gathered and transmitted to the capsule. Also based in California was a relief crew who would track down and retrieve the balloon and bring the pilots safely home.

There was no knowing where their landing site would be, but given the speed and flow of the jet stream, it seemed likely they would land in the San Francisco area or in the Nevada desert. In the end, though they might be aiming for the west coast of America, it was all in the hands of the God of the Winds. I tried not to let my imagination carry me too far ahead.

On Sunday, we drank green tea in our Japanese hotel room. The weather outside was very cold but still, the clear sky ablaze with the sun coming up over the mountains surrounding the sleepy little town.

✈

The next day we were back at the launch site. When nobody was around, I crept into the cramped capsule to see how these two pilots would manage together during their three to four sleepless nights. I left behind a small mascot with a bon voyage note attached. Perhaps it might help them stay safe.

At the press conference outside the operations room, it was announced that the adventurers hoped to leave on Tuesday 15 January. The mayor of Miyakonojo remarked that 15 January would be an apt day for the launch, as it was a traditional day of celebration for the young coming of age. Richard replied that indeed some people felt it was high time he and Per came of age!

As we were leaving, the mayor gave me a letter written by the local school children. Would I be sure it got on the capsule so Richard could hand it to the children of the nearest town when they landed? Of course I would! The idea of them landing safely and handing the letter to the children in America was indeed a happy thought!

✈

The next day, the weather was sunny and cold. For the launch to happen, our weatherman in California had to predict no wind on take-off, 200 miles per hour winds in the jet stream, and no wind on landing—not too much to ask!

When the weather conditions were optimum—meaning perfectly still—the Pacific Flyer would have to climb to its cruising altitude. The pilot would then have to manoeuver the balloon into the core of the jet stream, increasing their speed to 200 miles per hour.

By the next night things were looking good and we were all on standby as they began inflating cold air into the beautiful balloon. It was quite a party at the launch site, with food stalls lit up with Japanese lanterns, selling roasted octopus and Daikon, among many other treats.

At 3.00am, Richard and Per arrived and greeted the crowd before moving on to the site, now cleared of all spectators, to say goodbye to the ground staff. Before they entered the capsule, a runner dashed back to find Ted and me. Richard had asked for us.

As we said our emotional goodbyes, I knew I didn't dare look at Ted, for he would confirm the fear we both felt. Just as the capsule doors were about to close, I managed to remember to give Richard the children's letter as the mayor requested.

Now, with all the burners ablaze, we watched the capsule rise up into the air. We gaped and gasped as this vast illuminated balloon rose ominously into the sky. The crowd shouted and cheered but I can't say I shared their jubilance. I felt afraid of so very many unknowns.

Will Whitehorn, the project manager, dashed up to me: "Quick, come to the ops room! Richard wants to talk to you." I ran over and damn! In my nervous excitement I pressed the wrong button on the intercom! I heard Richard's voice as the Pacific Flyer started to drift away, but he never heard me respond, "We'll race you over—see you in America!"

✈

After collecting our suitcases, we had only an hour to make connections to a flight that would take us to San Francisco. The chase was on!

The atmosphere on the plane was tense and subdued. The silence was only broken when the captain came back to tell us that he heard from the operations crew that when Per and Richard had jettisoned their first empty gas bottle, two full bottles had also fallen away, leaving them now with only three to carry them over the Pacific. Gloom descended on all of us. The chief engineer began making calculations and cheered us up when he said that there just might be enough fuel left to complete the crossing.

Later, the captain came back again, this time to report that communication had been lost with the Pacific Flyer. Innocent and optimistic, I thought he meant that communication was broken off only with our aircraft and Richard and Per were still in touch with the ground ops in either Japan or San Francisco. Relieved at this notion, I fell asleep. I found out later that they had been out of communication with everyone for seven hours.

We welcomed the news at breakfast that the ground crew had managed to contact the Pacific Flyer once more and learned they were moving at a 200-mile-per-hour clip—they had crossed the dateline. I felt sure they were going to make it! We landed at San Francisco Airport to find a bus waiting to take us to the hotel, where we met up with Lindy, Vanessa and Penni. But before we could settle in, we were told to leave our suitcases in our room and get down to the lobby in five minutes. The balloon was travelling much faster than expected, so before we knew it, we were off again!

✈

Within minutes, Ted and I were whisked away by Learjet to Seattle. En route, we heard that flight control had advised Per and Richard to come out of the jet stream to conserve fuel—the sun was giving them enough solar power. Super news!

We were still on board at 3.50am when we heard that the balloon was expected to land at 9am somewhere between Canada's Great Bear Lake and Great Slave Lake. But when we landed to refuel, our pilot said he didn't have the necessary charts to make the flight. We tried not to panic. Will Whitehorn saved the day by contacting Virgin headquarters in London and asking them to fax charts showing the Northwest Territories and Alaska. By 6.30am we were in flight again, accompanied by a few journalists.

By 7.14am we heard that the Pacific Flyer was over the Rockies, now looking to land about 150 miles from the village of Yellowknife, Canada. They were making 107 knots and descending. Thank God!

On landing at Yellowknife in heavy snow, we found the hangar doors securely closed. Cold and shivering, we rang the bell and the owner appeared, looking a bit surprised to see Ted and me in summer attire. He was even more surprised when we said we'd come to find our son who'd flown over from Japan in a balloon!

"Well you'd better come in," was all he could say, looking us up and down. Will had chartered a small helicopter and invited us to join him, but we felt he had enough to worry about without Richard's parents in the chase. So Ted and I hired our own helicopter, which we shared with a reporter from the *Daily Mirror*. We were grateful for any transportation in this remote area, but I must say, this helicopter was the most antiquated machine I'd ever seen!

By 8am we heard that Richard and Per were now at 1,250 feet and descending. It was 20 degrees in Yellowknife, so we hitched a ride into town to buy gloves, hats and snow boots. I purchased some food, too, as I imagined Richard and Per would be hungry when they landed. Finally, I borrowed some clean hankies, remembering the First Aid I'd learned in my Star Girl training.

At 8.49am, we got word on the radio that the balloon might be landing in only 15 minutes. Would we be in time to find them in this desolate land with a snowstorm whirling about us? Our helicopter tried to follow Will's, which was in front of us. In icy cold and near blizzard conditions, we chopped over barren tundra, with only matchsticks of trees and a few frozen lakes interrupting the bright white snow.

I didn't have a headset so I did not really understand what was happening. Were we looking for the capsule or the balloon? Our eyes were glued to the white landscape below, the snow now heavy on the ground. I worried whether we'd even be able to spot the white capsule in the snow!

Our helicopter was so old that the door, with its rusty hinges, did not close properly. I don't think I have ever felt so cold. Ted tried to wedge an old newspaper between me and the door, but there was only so much one could do—we were flying through a Canadian snowstorm in the dead of winter, after all.

Finally we landed alongside the other helicopter. Silence. No one stirred for ten minutes; we just listened to the sound of the blades whirling. What was happening? Somewhere over the vast frozen Canadian barrens, between us and the Arctic Circle was a hot air balloon that had set out 46 hours earlier from southern Japan. Now it was lost in this impenetrable storm.

Our pilot descended from the helicopter to clean the windscreen, which was covered with ice that obscured his view. The other helicopter took off and we followed, though we didn't know where.

The windscreen iced over yet again so we landed once more. I handed the pilot a credit card, which he used to scrape the ice away. We took off again, by now having lost contact with the other helicopter. We tried to take photos of our position, lest we too were lost, but our cameras had ceased to work in the intense cold.

Ted, who had the only headset, took it off and shouted to me: "We're turning back. It's freezing to such a degree they can't get the spare fuel out to us and we've barely enough to get back to base."

What with a blizzard, a gap in the door and the windscreen wipers not working, we had to land again out on the tundra. Spiky pine trees protruded out of the snow – snow, snow, everywhere, but not a human to be seen. We soon realized that we would no longer be able to help in the search for the capsule, as there was now a real danger that we might get lost in the wilderness ourselves.

We managed to make it back to the heliport in Yellowknife after about 2pm. There Ted and I were immediately told that there had been no contact with the balloon for the past two hours. We were ushered out of the hangar and into a car, then driven to see the sights of Yellowknife. Bloody hell, what were we doing touring this town at a time like this, when I hadn't any idea when—or if—I'd see my son again?

Ted kept up a polite conversation with the driver but I was getting frantic. I needed to get to a telephone! We were taken to the heliport owner's house for a cup of tea. A cup of tea! Something stronger would have been more helpful. I asked if I could use the telephone but then wondered who I should ring. Penni, of course!

"Penni, Penni!" I shouted. "What's happening? We've been sent off for a cup of tea, of all things! I want to know what's going on."

"Leave it to me," she shouted back. "Give me your number and I'll ring you back."

I continued to nervously sip my tea while Ted dutifully kept up a conversation.

The telephone rang and I leapt for it. It was Will from the Great Slave Heliport, saying that both the balloon pilots had landed safely and had been in contact with the rescue helicopter that was searching for them. Richard had radioed: "We're okay but it's cold! Can you get us a taxi?" They had landed on a frozen plateau some 200 miles northwest of Yellowknife, with no injuries, thank God. The Canadian search and rescue professionals were on the case. We breathed a huge sigh of relief—at last we knew we'd see Richard and Per again very soon.

✈

The next day we found our way back to the hangar to greet them. There was no sweeter sound than the rescue helicopter blades churning slowly to a halt before the iced-up doors slowly opened and out came Richard and Per. The sheer joy of seeing them alive and well was overwhelming; tears have rarely poured from my eyes as they did at that moment.

Then the magnitude of their accomplishment hit me. They had flown a third of the way around the world and stayed airborne for 46 hours to become the first hot air balloon crew to cross the Pacific!

With hugs and kisses all around and flashes from a press photographer, the staff from the heliport looked somewhat bewildered, still not quite grasping the fact that these two men had flown in a balloon all the way from Japan. Yet somehow, out of nowhere, champagne appeared and was enjoyed by all!

When I saw that the heliport owner had brought along his two children, I was reminded of the letter from the children of Miyakonojo.

"Richard, I suppose you haven't managed to bring that letter from the Japanese kids?" I asked. My God, he'd remembered! He handed the well-travelled message to the two youngsters, making good on the mayor's hope that children across the Pacific would form a friendship with the children of his fair city. What a lovely, simple gesture that was—and a profound reminder of the warm human ties that bind us.

CHAPTER 11

Helping others through my charity work has always been
a great source of joy for me. A few short months after Richard's
Pacific crossing, Ted and I found ourselves in Hong Kong,
looking out a window on the top floor of the Regent Hotel at a
stretch of water teeming with Chinese junks, sampans, tugs and
ferries.

We were the guests of the late Oliver Foot, one of the founders
of ORBIS International, a charity dedicated to fighting blindness in
developing countries by providing surgical training to eye doctors
around the world. Incredibly, this training is carried out in a DC-
10 jet that has been converted into a mobile hospital. Realising the
charity's enormous benefit, Richard was providing complimentary
Virgin flights to volunteer doctors from the U.S. and Europe. As a
result, Ted and I were invited to visit the ORBIS aircraft and see its
amazing medical staff at work in Rangoon, Burma, which is now
called Myanmar.

✈

At the time of our visit, no foreigners or tourists had been allowed
into Burma since 18 September 1988. However, we had obtained a
visa through ORBIS by invitation of a Burmese colonel who was

also the Minister of Health. From the moment we touched down, we were given a royal welcome. The Burmese thought anyone connected with ORBIS must be angels from heaven. Indeed the ORBIS team was a heavenly lot but little did they realise Ted and I were no angels!

It was handshakes all round before we were swept off in a smart limo with Army and police cars leading the way, with two motorbike patrols on either side. Our driver took us to the Inya Lake Hotel, passing hundreds of bicyclists and pedestrians as we raced along. On this trip, we learned what it was like to be royalty, for this was how we were treated throughout our week in Burma.

✈

On the day after our arrival, Ted and I joined the ORBIS team of doctors, nurses and technicians in a military aircraft to fly to the picturesque city of Mandalay. Bicycles were everywhere, some with sidecars carrying passengers holding umbrellas to shield themselves from the sun in the 100-degree heat. We drove out to a rural area, passing wooden and thatched houses on stilts. We passed monks dressed in vivid saffron robes, women in pale pink and red robes and children in rust-coloured garb.

Finally we arrived at a Community Health Centre where health workers expressed their gratitude to the ORBIS team for restoring sight to two of the local inhabitants on their last visit. One of these was a weaver who, thanks to her eye surgery, could see again and was thus able to work and support her family.

The other success story was a leprosy worker who had gone totally blind. After an ORBIS operation had restored his vision, he was back on his bicycle, visiting lepers in the villages nearby. Though there was very little leprosy in Burma, we learned that it commonly caused blindness, and treatment required a corneal transplant, an operation ORBIS was teaching the local doctors, using closed-circuit television from inside the aircraft.

We then visited the crowded Mandalay Eye and ENT Hospital, where beds lined every corridor. Somewhat amazed by the sight of so many foreigners, the quietly suffering patients were happy to learn that these visitors were doctors and nurses who were there to help them.

On ORBIS missions, only a few patients are chosen from the many that need surgery in each host country. In Mandalay, 200 patients were screened for the four surgical slots. It's heartbreaking to see people turned away, but only the most effective teaching cases are selected. The goal is that the local doctors and nurses, who observe the operations by closed-circuit TV, will use the techniques they learn on other patients after ORBIS leaves. We were glad to learn that ORBIS follows up every visit by sending local medical personnel a collection of educational videos about the treatment of blindness caused by glaucoma, cataracts, malnutrition and leprosy.

Later in our first day in Burma, the Colonel Surgeon gave us a tour of a 700-bed military hospital built by the British in the 1930's. Given the strict military discipline in Burma, all the patients, however ill, sat up and saluted the Colonel Surgeon as we passed.

While viewing the hospital, we met a young Chinese doctor who took us to see his own newborn, just five days old and wrapped in a white blanket. The doctor mentioned that he and his wife had not yet found a name for the child so I said, "What better name than Oliver?" after ORBIS founder Oliver Foot. He and his wife liked the name and agreed! I hoped the child would follow in his father's footsteps and become a doctor, continuing the humanitarian legacy of Oliver Foot in Burma.

✈

With full police escort on 23 March, we returned to the military hospital where we were introduced to an American volunteer doctor who had just flown in from West Virginia. He would provide lectures, advice and surgery in his capacity as an oculoplastic surgeon. A second volunteer doctor, a glaucoma specialist, was visiting from British Columbia. He told us there were only 56 ophthalmologists in Burma, all eager to learn surgical techniques from the outside world.

We then met the director of the hospital, who walked us down the corridors full of patients who had been previously screened for surgery. Some had walked for miles, escorted by their family, hoping to be one of the lucky ones treated by the ORBIS team.

Outside each examining room, patients quietly awaited their verdict, while mothers anxiously held their babies, many of whom were blind or had eye tumours. In one room we waited to hear whether one child with a large tumour in one eye would be chosen. If so, the surgeons would have to remove the eye with the tumour, as it was affecting his vision in the other. One room we visited was for patients with glaucoma and another was for cataract patients. The queues in the corridor seemed to grow by the minute.

Before joining the ORBIS nurses who were lecturing to the Burmese nurses and matrons, an ORBIS volunteer told me the most moving story of a Burmese lady who had just approached her, pushing her way past the waiting patients. She was gently reprimanded, but the woman explained to the volunteer that she had walked many, many miles to thank the ORBIS team personally. She was a midwife who had gone blind, and ORBIS had performed an operation on her that enabled her to work again. Her gratitude knew no bounds. She came to present her clean bill of health and to say she was again able to deliver babies!

The 24th of March was a day to remember. We were whisked off to see the ORBIS team operating in the fully equipped surgical suite inside the DC-8 aircraft parked at Rangoon Airport. The plane sat alone in the hot sunshine, shiny white and clean, identified only by the ORBIS symbol on the tail—an eye encased in a globe and one simple Red Cross.

The first-class section of the plane had been converted into a classroom with 20 seats, now occupied by Burmese doctors intently studying the closed-circuit television screens. They were viewing a glaucoma operation that was taking place in the surgical suite in the centre section of the aircraft, with commentary by the American surgeon. In front of the doctors were microphones so they could ask the surgeon questions during the course of the operation.

We donned sterilised operating overalls, hats and booties and then passed through the recovery room where there were three patients resting in various stages of recovery, each tended by a nurse. From there we went into the instrument room, where we gingerly opened a door to witness the glaucoma surgery still in progress in the operating arena. I wondered for a moment whether I would faint but I managed to hold steady.

I was fascinated to see two anaesthetists working side by side, one Swedish, one British. A surgeon from Canada was assisted by a Burmese surgeon and a staff ophthalmologist from Columbia was teaching a Burmese nurse. A video of the procedure would later be sent to the various Burmese hospitals with commentary by the surgeons.

The next day, Ted and I visited the oldest monk in Burma, a 96-year-old man who was famous for his teachings and writings. As we sat cross-legged on the floor in front of him, we listened, awestruck, to every word this old monk was saying. His voice was so quiet that we found ourselves shuffling closer and closer, not wanting to miss a word. He told us about how an ORBIS surgeon had operated on his cataracts, enabling him to see again. Like many of the other Buddhists Ted and I had met in our lives, the man seemed to exude a sense of tranquillity we don't often see in the West.

✈

The next morning we visited the ORBIS plane again to see the results of the previous day's surgeries.

The little child we had seen at the screening had just been operated on for his tumour. On enquiring about the result, the nurses answered that all was fine; the tumour was benign. They introduced us to the child's mother, who was sitting at his bedside in the recovery room, smiling a radiant smile.

I later heard that this operation had taken an unusual turn. The story was related to me by the aircraft's mechanic, who said he was busy checking the wheels under the aircraft when a nurse rushed down, asking him urgently to send up a drill.

"What size?" he answered.

"Send them all!" she answered. He promptly obliged, and the surgeon selected the size he needed, had it sterilized and proceeded to drill through the child's bone to remove the tumour. The Burmese doctors in the audience were rightly astounded—as were we!

✈

At a private dinner that evening below the Golden Pagoda, a magnificent tower of glittering gold studded with jewels, our host—the retired former director general of the local hospital—kept us very amused.

He mentioned that his house was huge, far too big for him and his wife. He went on to explain that he had managed to fill it up with animals and reptiles. "Oh, please explain more," we urged, though we strained a little to understand his English.

"Well, the frogs and toads live in the sink."

"But how do you wash?" I asked.

"We take no notice, and anyhow they like the water."

"What else?"

"There are two large dogs, lots of sparrows, a squirrel and, of course, a long fat snake that lives mostly on our bedroom ceiling."

"What does the snake eat—the toads?" I asked, smiling.

"Oh, no," he replied. "They get on very well together; the snake eats the sparrows, but I don't mind as they wake me up with their chatter every morning at 4am."

By now we would believe anything. I made a mental note to send him the book I was reading about an Englishman travelling through India on an elephant—our host and this man were two of a kind!

While we were enjoying dinner, the rest of the ORBIS team was back at the hospital, lecturing, listening and discussing patients and their conditions. What a wonderful team, having started at 8am and still working at 10.30pm. They were indeed "flying angels."

✈

On our final day, a Burmese man approached us and, seeing my ORBIS tee-shirt, he embraced me, with tears streaming down his cheeks. Somewhat taken aback, I learned he was another grateful patient who had walked for a day through the jungle to reach the ORBIS team who restored his eyesight. He was determined to thank each volunteer in person!

We spent the morning at the hospital with a Mongolian ophthalmologist who was giving a post-op clinic. This was surely the highlight of our week, as these were the patients whose sight had been restored—a few of them could see for the first time in their lives. This group included a student whose eyesight had been damaged by a stone that was thrown at him—he thought he would never be able to study or work again.

Then there was the seven-year-old boy who was born with congenital glaucoma and had been entirely blind from birth. We watched in anticipation while the nurse slowly removed his bandages. Gradually he realised there was a new world around him and he ran, touching everything he could lay his hands on. We cried to see the child's elation as he kissed and hugged his mother and father and little sister, finally able to see them for the first time.

In the adjoining room, there was a 10-year-old boy who had never had been to school because he had cataracts in both eyes. The ORBIS team managed to operate successfully on one eye (the other had gone too far), so now he would be able to attend school and play with the other children. He, too, was ecstatic!

Finally, in walked a very pretty girl. Before surgery, her eyelids had drooped heavily over her eyes and she had been unable to see unless she tilted her head back. Now she could see normally and she stood proudly before us, smiling and thanking ORBIS for her new life.

Ted and I left Burma with the highest respect for ORBIS and its dedicated team. I was very sad to hear, many years later, that their devoted leader Oliver Foot died of a heart attack in his early 60's, but was glad to learn that ORBIS is still going strong, restoring hope and sight around the world.

CHAPTER 12

IN THE LATE SPRING OF 1991, Ted and I hosted a flower festival at Cakeham for the benefit of the local hospital and an organization supporting research into cystic fibrosis, a muscular deterioration that causes children to die before they reach the age of 20.

Little did I know what would be involved when I happily volunteered our home as a venue. Everything had to be removed from much of the house to make room for 193 different flower arrangements. During the set-up and the event itself, Ted and I moved into a room in the back of the house where we remained, hidden in our bolt hole, whilst 300 viewers toured our home for two days. The house looked superb, with magnificent flowers absolutely everywhere, even draped around the bathroom taps, and the scent was intoxicating. Flowers even overflowed into the chapel—the Bishop of Chichester would have been most impressed!

The sun shone at its best all day and even the mallard—as if on cue—appeared from behind the bushes, followed by her eight little ducklings. This put the final touch on a very successful festival for the spectators who drifted around our house and grounds.

To our delight, the flower festival generated £7,000. That sum provided a nice-sized donation to the not-for-profit and enabled the hospital to purchase two heart pumps. The manufacturer also got in the spirit and donated another. This result was gratifying to us, as it exceeded all our expectations!

That summer was fun, especially when we welcomed Lindy, Robin, Otto, Milo and Ludo to Cakeham to celebrate my birthday.

The children were all awake and ready to play at 6.30am—they explored room after room, pulling out any toys they could find. Not four months earlier, Vanessa had given birth to another son, Louis, bringing our grandchildren total to 10!

Yes, 12 July was my day. Face up to reality, I told myself. Born in 1924, that made me 68 years old—good heavens, that sounded great! Thank goodness I could still bend in all directions, play a damn good game of tennis and ride my bike furiously with very few aches and pains. (My secret was taking one Selenium ACE and one odourless garlic capsule a day, whilst keeping busy and active.)

I had a fantastic day. Lindy cooked breakfast. Then Ludo, Milo and Otto told me there was a surprise for me outside but I would have to be blindfolded. They led me down to the stables (a somewhat precarious walk, especially when led by the little people) with Lindy whispering, "For God's sake, boys, look where you're going under that scaffolding!"

At last they stopped, pressed a key into my hand and removed the blindfold. There before me was a muddy, old tractor. "All yours!" they shouted, before spinning me round and pointing to a shiny new white Honda Civic, a present from Rick. The world was safer with me in a Civic, I promise. I had once ridden that old tractor and managed to flip it upside down after getting tangled up in a backyard swing!

✈

One of the highlights of my 68th year was attending the inaugural flight of the DC3 Dakota plane from Orlando to Key West, the first craft to fly for Richard's newest airline, Vintage Airways. This plane had originally been used in World War II to carry American troops over from England to Normandy for the landings, and it was to be my namesake.

After five years of following Richard around the world on his various challenges, from America to the Scilly Isles, from Maine to Ireland and from Japan to Canada, I looked forward to my own little adventure, with none of the hair-raising thrills that were typical of Richard's exploits!

When Richard had phoned to say "Pack your bags, we're off to Orlando and then on to Key West," of course I jumped to pack my bag. "You are about to help me launch a new airline and the first plane will be called Eve," he explained. "It's an old classic Dakota DC3," he added, "so would you please look for your old uniform?"

The pressure was on. I had one week to search cupboards and attics for my skirt, blouse, hat and handbag—and even my old BSAA stewardess badge!

✈

There was no fear and trepidation this time as Ted and I boarded a Virgin 747 at Gatwick. We were presented with a press release on the details of our trip and the history of the old twin-propeller DC3 Dakota that was about to start carrying Florida tourists. Valued more for nostalgia than for high-tech efficiency, these planes were known for their safety and comfort and were reverently referred to as "the gentleman's aircraft."

I was intrigued to learn a bit about Eve's history. This old Dakota DC3 had played a pivotal role in the Allied victory in World War II. Later it had been bought by a Canadian group to supply the oil pipeline in Alaska. In 1980, its undercarriage collapsed and for several years it languished on a runway in Spokane, Washington. Finally, in 1989, it was completely rebuilt and regained its full flying certificate.

Since then, the two DC3s that formed the Virgin Airtours operation—Eve and her sister craft, Amelia Earhart—had been upgraded to modern standards with up-to-date navigation and communication equipment, air conditioning, and stereo systems.

The interiors of these planes were completely refurbished with wooden panelling and enlarged windows that enabled the 28 passengers to view panoramas of the land and the sparkling water below. The planes would fly at 2,000 feet, averaging 160 miles per hour.

After a quick overnight at the Hyatt Regency Hotel in Orlando on 2 December, I prepared for the launch by donning my old, moth-eaten air hostess uniform. Richard was in authentic 1940s attire, including a double-breasted jacket and Oxford bags, and his hair was smoothed back in a sharp style.

Ted and I climbed into a Rolls convertible driven graciously by our chauffeur, who was, of course, Richard himself! We proceeded slowly through Orlando, seeing puzzled looks on the faces of everyone we passed, who were no doubt wondering what the hell was going on!

At the little Orlando airport, we were greeted by friends, reporters and snap-happy cameramen. The excitement was building as Richard drove Ted and me across the tarmac. As we neared the Dakota, newly painted and sparkling in the hot sunshine, Richard shouted, "Where are the brakes on this thing?"

Ted and I froze, thinking not only of the pending damage to the valuable Rolls but also to my plane! Whether or not Richard was joking, he did eventually find the brakes, and just in time. So much for our stress-free adventure. We alighted safely to break the champagne bottle over one of the two propellers of this ageless beauty. Our pilot greeted us, dressed in World War II flying gear, a true "Biggles" with goggles and flying jacket.

Next to Eve was Amelia, also smartly painted white with red stripes along the body and a red-tipped nose and tail. Amelia was to fly alongside us. Whilst the two engines were revving up and the passengers were enjoying the musical hits from the 1940s such as "In the Mood" and "As Time Goes By," there was a commotion at the rear of the aircraft. Skip, a well-trained brown Labrador, had bounded up the gangway to the cockpit. The pilot reprimanded his mascot and Skip duly retreated, looking somewhat forlorn. The flight attendant, also dressed in a uniform inspired by the 1940s, explained that dogs had been popular flying companions for pilots during that period.

During the maiden flight that lasted just under two hours, it felt like we crossed the threshold of time. Richard served us champagne and we cooled ourselves with wooden fans, on the back of which were the emergency landing instructions. There were original magazines from the era—*Life*, *Look*, the *Saturday Evening Post*, and *Everybody's Magazine*—that truly brought us back to the golden age of flying.

Our short flight ended at Key West, the southernmost spot in the Continental United States. An old wood-panelled trolley bus took us to the Pier House Hotel, a seaside hotel surrounded by a jungle of hibiscus, palms, plumbago and abundant bizzie-lizzies.

The following day Ted and I decided to sail off on Segago, a 56ft catamaran, to an uninhabited island where we swam and snorkelled amongst the coral reef. That evening we wandered through the old tobacco town, drifting down to the beach to salute the sunset, a Key West tradition. There was a street market on the water's edge offering every entertainment imaginable: jugglers, fire eaters, a modern Houdini in chains, sword swallowers and even performing cats.

The glowing red sun was disappearing but still bright enough to glorify the silhouette of the old sailing boats. Suddenly, to our amazement, the two old Dakotas, Eve and Amelia, swooped down from the sky directly in front of us. As they disappeared from sight, I recalled the words of a pilot who once said, "The best replacement for a DC3 is another DC3!"

CHAPTER 13

REMEMBER 1993 BEING FULL TO the brim with family commotion. In January we visited Vanessa and Robert, who were staying in Los Angeles for a few months. Soon after we arrived, we were up early one morning to walk our grandson Noah to school, surely an unusual sight for passing limos carrying those Americans who were not accustomed to walking! Noah was named VIP in his class for the week, so he asked me to give a talk to his 30 classmates. Sitting in a kid's chair to face them was a surprisingly daunting prospect. I started by explaining my relationship to Noah and then went on to explain how we'd come all the way over from England. During question time I asked: "How do you think we got here?" I'd hoped to hear a chorus of "On a Virgin plane!" But no, one keen little boy at the back piped up to say, "On the Mayflower, Miss!"

✈

In early June, I attended the Southern Writers Conference in Earnley, listening closely to every word as other attendees and I shared our work with well-known writers. I enjoyed being in the company of others who took pleasure in putting pen to paper and made some lovely friends there.

I had written a few children's stories and was in the middle of writing a novel, tentatively titled *Lara*, about a young woman facing a life crisis. At the time I was afraid to send it out in case it was rejected, but I still loved working on it and my other writing projects too. In later years, I had my secretaries send out my writing, and though several of my travel articles were published in newspapers, my novels and stories could not find a home—publishers didn't seem to like them. I've also met various book agents in the UK and abroad who were quick to promise they could help me publish my work, but my hopes were dashed every time. Never mind—no one could take the lifetime of joy and satisfaction my writing has given me! For me, writing is like a friend I can count on.

✈

In early summer, Vanessa, Lindy, Richard and their respective spouses went off to celebrate Vanessa and Robert's 10th anniversary on Shona, their island retreat on the west coast of Scotland. Ted and I were left to entertain all the grandchildren at Cakeham for the weekend. Imagine the chaos when two carloads of grandchildren arrived on Friday at lunchtime!

Ted organised bicycles and sleeping bags and the garden was soon alive with the eight bigger children careening around on bikes, while the smaller ones tried to keep up on the various wheelie toys we had for them. Meanwhile in the house, we prepared bedrolls and meals for the whole gang. It was wonderful to be grandparents to those 10 grandchildren, but we doubted the weekend would end without incident.

Sure enough, seven-year-old Sam managed to slip away and sit on our front wall, throwing apples at passing cars. This must have seemed like great fun until an enraged driver showed up at our front door, demanding an apology. Sam was sorry and apologized to the driver and later to us, understanding that he was playing a dangerous game for those trying to keep their eyes on the road. We hoped he'd learned his lesson. In any case, Ted and I were both quite relieved when our child-sitting weekend was over!

✈

We did love being with our grandchildren and treasured our time with each of them. At the end of July, we cared for Lindy's boys for a week while she was in London for work. We took Jack and Otto to the Itchenor Junior Fortnight, a famous racing series event organised by the Itchenor Sailing Club that has given many famous yachtsmen and women their start. One such beneficiary was Stewart Morris, who won the gold medal for England, and Christina Bassadone, who was chosen to race in the International Fourteens for the Olympics.

The boys were anxious to try out their new boat, Yogi, a secondhand "mirror" we'd recently bought for them at Itchenor. We spent an enjoyable week watching 12-year-old Jack as skipper and 9-year-old Otto as crew, racing Yogi both morning and afternoon. The weather was pretty boisterous but all went well until they floundered on the mud and had to be towed back to the harbour. Then, to add insult to injury, a sudden gust came up, and over they went!

I watched this spectacle through my field glasses and ran back to the Yacht Club as the rescue boat delivered the two boys to dry land. Jack had to be carried up the jetty; he was hyperventilating and complaining of a pain in his head. A doctor urged us to take him immediately to hospital.

It was an emotional ride to the hospital and Ted and I were terribly worried. But Jack's x-rays appeared in order and he was allowed to leave. Phew! After only a day of recuperating, he was back at racing again. I later learned that if someone is hyperventilating, one can stop the process by giving them a brown paper bag to breathe into. After that experience, I added that item to my First Aid kit!

✈

After working on my novel for several months, I finished in December at last. It just needed another edit for final correction and then I dreamed it might someday be published. But there was no time for editing just yet, as we were off with Joan to Toulouse, where we would pick up the new Virgin Airbus and return the next day to be welcomed by Princess Diana. We would be just in time, as the day before, she had made the announcement that she was retiring from public life.

When we arrived at Heathrow, the Airbus was towed into a hangar for the dedication ceremony. Richard escorted Princess Diana up to the dais, where he spoke to the crowd. Diana's vivid green outfit provided a rich contrast to the smart red uniforms of the Virgin air hostesses. When she parted the curtain covering the name of the aircraft, singer Chris de Burgh sang "The Lady in Red". The £67 million aircraft would be Virgin's first Airbus.

The moment was so perfectly timed and conducted that I turned to Ted and said, "I'm proud."

Later we flew in the Airbus to Gatwick with Princess Diana, Richard and Joan, first sweeping low over Aerospace in Bristol in recognition of their brilliant wing design, then flying low over Windsor Castle where Diana pointed below and said with a smile, "That's Granny's house!"

✈

The whole family loved music so my next Christmas gift to everyone was a second-hand Zimmerman baby grand piano. The family took turns playing it and even I was trying to learn, spending every spare minute practicing. Vanessa started learning, as did the twins, Milo and Ludo, who sat side by side, four hands playing simultaneously. I found it somewhat awkward to play, with only four good fingers on my left hand and only one and a half on my right, thanks to my boating accident. But I kept struggling with beginners' music and was content to try and work out the notes!

A phone call from Penni at Rick's office interrupted one of my practice sessions. Would I consider dressing up in my old WREN uniform to receive an award on Richard's behalf at the Royal Albert Hall? This award, given in honour of Winston Churchill, was bestowed the English citizens who have done the most to make England great—what an honour for Richard, and what an honour for me to represent him! I was delighted to say yes.

The big night arrived and I nervously waited alone in a plush red velvet-covered box with only my nerves for company. I was wondering whether I should help myself to a drink at the small bar set-up I spied nearby when there was a knock at the door, alerting me that it was my turn to step forward. My head held high, but feeling quite shaky inside, I walked the entire circumference of the huge hall en route to the stage.

About halfway around, I was joined by the beautiful Rebecca Stephens, who was receiving her award as the first British woman to climb Mount Everest. She put me at ease by telling me there was nothing to fear. I thanked her and when I reached the rostrum, with arc lights glaring down at me, I managed to deliver a brief thank you speech on Richard's behalf before being presented with a bronze bust of Winston Churchill.

✈

In May, Ted and I joined the inaugural Virgin flight from Heathrow to San Francisco. One of the main attractions for us was seeing the small island of Alcatraz where some of America's most notorious criminals were housed until the facility closed in 1964. It became a national museum open to tourists who arrived in droves by ferry to ponder the misery that the prisoners within must surely have endured.

It reminded me of Robben Island in South Africa, where Nelson Mandela was incarcerated for 18 years. He's been not only my hero but Richard's too, along with the many thousands worldwide who recognise his greatness.

✈

People often say birthdays seem to come faster as one gets older—it's true. Suddenly I was 70—wow! What a day. Ted gave me gorgeous pearl drop earrings and the promise of an electric Sinclair motor for my bike. I stopped in at the Virgin office in London, where I had been working a few days a week on various projects, and was surprised to find bouquets of flowers with lovely notes from the different Virgin branches. Yes, it felt good to be 70 years old. Two of my local friends, Katie Byre and Jilly Haywood, announced that their present was to prepare a celebratory dinner for 60 guests who had been invited to Cakeham. Friends from my early dancing days, from our days at Tanyards and from the area around Cakeham all attended, and what a party it was!

I had one more birthday surprise in store: a few weeks after my big day, Richard provided the family with tickets to Necker Island. Gathering there each year to celebrate three July birthdays—Joan's, Richard's and mine—was one of my favourite family rituals. This year, along with our children and grandchildren, we were joined by my 96-year-old mother and my sister Clare. We had a glorious time and I looked forward to watching the family grow and prosper as I set my sights on 80!

CHAPTER 14

I N THE SPRING OF 1995, Ted and I decided to invite our 11 grandchildren, including Vanessa's new baby Ivo, to stay with us at Cakeham again, giving their parents the opportunity to spend another holiday together. Cakeham came alive as they all dashed around. Then Sam decided to construct a bow and arrow whilst Milo, Ludo and Otto were busy launching our rubber boat in the lake. Sam took aim at Milo, and to his amazement the arrow worked. Shrieks brought me running, only to find Milo with blood pouring from his eye. A stitch at the Chichester Hospital sorted him out easily enough. Sam had learnt a hard lesson and we were all relived that Milo was fine. Ted and I, meanwhile, had sprouted a few more grey hairs!

✈

We were summoned to London in July for an important press announcement, though Richard had already shared the news with us. The Virgin Global Balloon Challenge would be his most dangerous and most daring undertaking yet. I did not relish what was to come.

We joined the press in the lecture hall of the National Maritime Museum in Greenwich. Richard and Per announced that they were planning to take off in November when they would catch the jet stream with the hope of circling the globe. Their balloon—a modern version of one pioneered by Jean-Francois Pilâtre de Rozier over 200 years ago—would be propelled with a combination of helium and propane burners and would be capable of staying aloft for 21 days.

They explained that their capsule would be slung below a 250ft high balloon flying at 30,000 feet. The greatest dangers were ice adhering onto the balloon at high altitude and forcing them down, or hurricanes blowing them off course and forcing the balloon down in the middle of the Himalayas where there was little chance of rescue. Ted and I filed out of the hall silently whilst the reporters' voices rose behind us as they called their editors with the news.

✈

Ted and I decided to put Richard and his balloon scheme out of our minds for the moment to enjoy the summer and to spend time with our new Golden Retriever puppy, Suki, who romped everywhere and came with us on short trips away from home.

Day after day the temperatures were in the 90s with clear blue skies and calm seas. Still, there was enough wind for Lindy's five boys to excel in their various boats—they were becoming quite expert at windsurfing and participated once more in Itchenor Junior Fortnight. Two weeks of various races concluded with an evening of parties, barbecues, discos, tennis and even crab races for the younger ones. Prizegiving was a proud day for us as we watched them all receive some recognition.

✈

As I always say, life moves on, and so it did for my next birthday, celebrated belatedly in August in Menorca. We were met by Lindy and the boys, who promptly blindfolded me and led to the family's red speedboat where Ted and I were sped around to Humble Pie, with cries of "Don't peek! You're looking!"

The blindfold was removed and behold! There tied up to our jetty was the most magnificent llout, a Majorcan fishing boat, with a magnum of champagne dangling from the stern. Oh, the excitement! I pressed one button and the anchor rose; I pressed another and down it went. There was certainly no lack of power with two large 75-horsepower diesel engines. Rick had been to the island earlier to try out various boats and had chosen this one, called by chance Eva. What a wonderful surprise!

✈

October is a good month to visit Italy and what with my longing to meet up with my old dancing friend Brenda and her Italian husband Raffaelo, a visit to Florence seemed the answer. She had met Raffaelo, a professional photographer, whilst dancing for a ballet company in Italy many years before, and ended up starting her own ballet school in Rome that eventually became one of the top schools in the country.

Both Brenda and Raffaelo were at the airport to meet us and we spent a wonderful week enjoying the beauty and history of Florence. We stayed in their flat, which was adorned with beautiful hand-painted murals on all the walls, and was situated opposite the famous Ponte Vecchio Bridge. How wonderful to have a reunion with one's childhood friend! We were both growing old but treasured our memories of years gone by, and what fond memories they were!

✈

Seeing Brenda made me stop for a moment to take stock of my life; I'm usually too busy making things happen to spend much time on reflection. And besides, writing gives me the time to reflect and be creative too. But as I looked ahead to 1996, I was thankful the family was in fine shape. Rick, Lindy, and Vanessa were happy, healthy, and busy. Ted, thank goodness, was doing well and all our grandchildren were super. As for me, I was thankful to be healthy and enjoyed my personal pastimes: writing every morning, playing tennis once a week and playing golf whenever the opportunity arose.

Though I had yet to find a publisher for *Lara*, I was working on another novel I'd tentatively titled *The Cruel Mountain*. I was also looking for a publisher for my children's story, *Sarky Puddleboat*. Agents said they liked it but no one could seem to get it into print.

It was such a hard road to have a published book in hand that maybe I should have come to my senses and taken up cookery instead!

✈

Soon after returning from Italy to chilly England, we accepted Richard's invitation to join him and his family for what would become one of my favourite holidays: an elephant and canoeing safari in sunny Zimbabwe. We packed cameras, sun cream, khaki shorts and field glasses and headed off to Heathrow with Richard, Joan, Holly, Sam, and a family friend, Dr. Tim Evans. We landed at Harare where we were met by some of Tim's family who took us to Charles Prince Airport nearby. We took off and enjoyed a clear view of Victoria Falls and after that, mile upon mile of scrub country.

After a one-hour flight, we were met by our host, John, who drove us another 25 miles through the Zambezi National Park to the Elephant Camp where we were to spend the next three days. The camp featured a few straw-roofed huts, a small swimming pool and a large watering hole to attract the wild animals; it felt like a private enclave.

We had no sooner eaten lunch and unpacked when we saw four elephants ambling towards us through the scrub, all in line, each with its keeper, known as a mahout, on its back. Named Miss Ellis, Jumbo, Jock, and Jack, they drank at the watering hole and then sauntered past us to their sturdy stables made of poles from the mopane tree. We watched John give them a training lesson for just under 15 minutes, the daily limit of their concentration. Unlike Indian elephants, African elephants weren't supposed to be trainable, but that didn't deter John. He lined them up and gave the command, "Good morning!" and was answered by delightful low rumbles. Next command, "Raise right foot!" and John would check their feet. Next was "Cross feet!" which they all performed perfectly.

"Heads up!" came next, which Jumbo performed particularly well, with his head high and his trunk tucked back in between his tusks. Each time they responded properly to a command, they were rewarded with a lump of dried molasses. "Two steps back!" John shouted and the elephants backed up. "Forward two steps!" he'd shout, and yes, they stepped forward!

Their keepers then threw down their prodders, which the elephants picked up with their trunks before handing them overhead to their mahout. Finally they were given the emergency command "Sit down!" This was a critical command if the mahouts found themselves in dangerous circumstances. At the end of their training session the elephants seemed happy to relax—and we too needed a rest.

After a peaceful afternoon spent sleeping and swimming, we were invited to ride the elephants ourselves. Jumbo's mahout, Monson, sat up in front, with me in the middle and Ted behind. Our feet rested on a long hollow bamboo strip that made a very comfortable stirrup.

Monson was most interesting to talk to as we rode along through the bare bush. The sun glowed red. A black-breasted snake eagle, one of the largest wing-spanned birds in the bush, soared above. The sound of doves and the red-billed hornbills echoed in the distance as we watched an inquisitive giraffe peer at us from over a tree whilst warthogs scurried past below.

Elephants live for 60 years or more and Monson told us proudly that Jumbo, now only 16, would be his for life. He also explained the many uses of the elephant's trunk. A versatile organ, the tip's fine sensory hairs are used as a snorkel, a hand, a baton, a winch, a vacuum cleaner, a sand blaster and, of course, a trumpet and a pocket pincher!

The next day Ted stayed at the camp and I went off on Jumbo with Monson and John. We meandered through the scrub, with very little green plant life in view save a wild crocus or two valiantly growing out of the rock. Even at 7am it was very hot, as deeper and deeper into the bush we went, with Jumbo's ears flapping back and forth, acting as a fan as he flicked flies away. Sometimes he would spray his body with the water stored in his trunk to cool off. Monson said the older elephants take in 120 litres of water a day, the younger ones about 100.

Lunch was a welcome sight indeed as we spotted the smoke from a fire and a picnic being set out under the butterfly-shaped leaves of a mopane tree. John suddenly shouted that he had spotted a large pack of wild dogs. Oh, boy! Leaving our cooks to prepare lunch, we set off in the Jeeps, our anticipation great, as wild dogs were seldom seen in the vicinity.

John led us through the bush, passing giraffe, impala, baboons and warthogs. The warthogs, the clowns of the bush, are my favourite wild animals, though they are not the most beautiful. Warts protrude below their eyes and above their small tusks and their tails stick bolt upright as a useful flag for their young to follow.

Arriving at the dam in the heat of the midday sun, we stopped abruptly when we saw 20 or more large vultures greedily eyeing a drowned kudu in the shallow water. We watched through our field glasses as the hyenas and vultures waited for dusk before picking at the unfortunate creature.

On our last day at the Elephant Camp, we were awakened by the nightjars' chorus in the bush surrounding our straw-covered hut. I needed to say goodbye to Jumbo, who by now I was quite convinced knew me. So after giving him the most succulent branch I could find, along with a tickle and a stroke, I joined the others for breakfast before we left for our next adventure, which was to paddle down the Zambezi River in light canoes.

✈

Taking off from a rough runway and flying along the vast expanse of Lake Kariba and over the Kariba Dam, we flew into the Zambezi Valley where we were met by Dave Christenson, a professional guide who proved to be an encyclopaedia of local knowledge during the next three days.

Binoculars, sun cream and hats were essentials as we were driven in an open Jeep through the Mana Pools National Park to our first camp. We bounced over the flat flood plains of bare grasses and barren trees, each bend revealing a variety of wild animals— monkeys, impala, kudus, elephants and finally, a scrawny guinea fowl who seemed unconcerned about which animals were likely to enjoy him for their next mouthful. Finally we stopped by the fast-flowing shallow river where we saw five flimsy-looking fibreglass canoes moored on the bank. Our exuberance dimmed a bit when we realized that they would be our only protection from the animals and the elements.

Dave lined us up on the riverbank and gave us sober instructions. "This is a dangerous safari. The biggest dangers of all will be the hippo, the crocodile and the lethal hidden stumps." He explained that the stumps were thin trees that had been mutilated by the river; hitting them would surely mean our canoes would tip over, most probably landing us in the mouth of the aforementioned crocodile!

There was one more danger to be avoided—having our canoes positioned between two buffalo on opposite banks of the river. "Before we get into our canoes," Dave warned, "there is an unwritten law in the African wilderness: Where there is something to eat, there is someone to eat it. Don't put yourselves on the menu."

Ted's back hurt after the bumpy ride, and I wondered how he was going to manage riding in a small canoe for three days. But there was no turning back now and nowhere else to go. Leaving two lions sleeping peacefully nearby, we climbed into our five canoes and gingerly started to paddle. Dave and Sam were in the lead canoe with us, with the others following in single file. Ted lightened the tension, saying I looked like Lady Stanley herself. "In that case," I answered, "I hope to find Dr. Livingston down river!"

Perhaps the most frightening moment of our three days was on the first bend where we encountered two cape buffalos, one on either side of the river. Wasn't this just the situation that Dave had told us to avoid?

The one on the nearer bank decided to charge at us. Young Sam, only four years old, looked up to see the massive body of this formidable bull buffalo angrily advancing. Exposing his large mouth, waving his tail and shaking his horns, he thundered toward our group. Dave, with a quick presence of mind, rose up, bashing the side of the canoe with his paddle and shouting unrepeatable words! The bull took fright and turned away, lucky for us. No need for Dave's gun this time. Phew! And Sam was unperturbed; he just smiled and accepted the episode as if it happened to him every day.

The currents on the Zambezi run at about five knots, so paddling along to its rhythm was not much of a hardship and gave us time to enjoy the floating platforms of purple water hyacinth near the river banks. The flat mud plains beyond were strewn with exotic birds— great white egrets, sacred ibis, fish eagles and small, vibrantly coloured malachites with red legs and bills somewhat similar to our kingfishers. On the riverbank, impalas pirouetted gracefully and kudus stood like statues nearby. With all this natural beauty, it was almost impossible to take a bad photograph.

We saw a herd of buffalo, seemingly peaceful as they grazed in the early morning light, suddenly kick up a cloud of dust. Minutes later Dave issued a sharp, urgent command: "Stop paddling! Keep still!" Dave's words were never to be taken lightly. Within seconds the buffalo were stampeding through the river. The enormous herd looked truly terrifying, a ghostly sight in the sandy haze as they thundered past us and disappeared into the bush.

Breathing a sigh of relief, we once more felt safe on the little expanse of river bed, in spite of the presence of impala and lions moving across the shallows as we glided past. The drought had made the wild animals feel stressed, so Dave was fearful of taking us too far away from the relative security of the riverbank.

At sunrise we stopped for a most welcome breakfast cooked on a barbeque grill by two guides who had travelled ahead by Jeep. After canoeing for three hours, we sat back devouring our sausages, happy and intrigued by the crocodiles in the river below. Their camouflage made it difficult to count just how many there were. Dotting the surface of the river were hippos with little humps and two gleeful eyes protruding above the water. Their extraordinary grunting and groaning left us wondering if it was pain or pleasure they were experiencing!

Braving the river once more, we continued our journey, accompanied by hornbills and the incessant honking of Egyptian geese. Our next stop was Chikwenya Island, where we stopped for a drink. We innocently assumed this would be a safe haven from wild animals, but that was not the case. From out of the bushes sauntered a huge bull elephant!

There was no running away. Dave ordered us to sit still and not utter a word—there was no escape for anyone. The elephant wandered nonchalantly to within about 20 feet of our party to enjoy the fallen nuts around us. How relieved we all were when he decided to stroll off and join two other large bulls.

Meanwhile, the advance party of Jeeps, cooks and porters had driven through the bush to erect the night tents. By the time dusk descended, we had paddled about 25 kilometres and were looking forward to settling in at our beautifully prepared campsite. The porters came down to the water's edge to help us land our canoes.

Tired but feeling elated about the events of the day, we went into our respective tents to collect our soap before returning outside for a quick wash in the canvas bowl. For anyone brave enough to venture further into the bush, there was a water tank the porters had erected hanging from a mopane tree behind a screen. Pull the string and bingo, you had a welcome shower!

Feeling refreshed, we all sat around the campfire to watch the glow of the sunset slipping slowly over the Zambian hills. Contrasting colours of reds, violets, vivid pinks, yellows and blues gave way to darkness, leaving just the sound of the river and the grunting hippos to remind us that we were guests of the wild.

We retired to our tents, gingerly feeling our way through the darkness, listening to the roar of a lion in the distance, praying there would be no need to spend a penny in the night. Peering through my mosquito netting, I saw a pack of hyenas prowling around, all laughing in a frenzy as they drank the milk for our early morning tea and ate our soap before digging through the rubbish bags. I decided my only hope was to dive under the bedclothes and send up a prayer.

After two more days in the wild, our river safari came to an end and we were flown back to Harare. Prior to this holiday, Ted had been having pain in his back. Now he was walking with no pain and feeling spry and healthy. So sitting astride an elephant and riding in a small canoe for over 100 miles must surely be the recommendation doctors should give their patients with aching backs!

CHAPTER 15

O NE EARLY JANUARY MORNING, PENNI called with a green alert—
we would be leaving the next morning for Marrakech, Morocco
via Paris.

Morocco was chosen as the launch site for Richard's around-
the-world balloon challenge because weather conditions there were
perfect for ballooning and the jet stream lay overhead. It was one of
the major aviation records still to be achieved and I knew Richard
could do it if he set his mind to it. I knew little about Morocco
before this trip and couldn't have guessed that it would become one
of my favourite places on earth.

And so it was that Ted and I, Lindy, Ned, Milo, Otto and Ludo,
along with half the world's media, technicians, photographers and,
of course, the balloon crew, found ourselves in a hotel in Marrakech
just beyond the sun-baked clay walls of the famous souk.

The weather was dry, warm and sunny as we waited, day after
day, for the jet stream winds to build up sufficiently to carry the
900,000-cubic-foot balloon around the world. We used the time to
explore the country and meet some of its lovely, generous people.

Wandering through the Medina in the hot sunshine was a noisy,
dusty, colourful experience; Arabs and a few Berbers were trying
to make a dirham or two in the large market square. There were
snake charmers, jugglers, old men extracting teeth, monkeys on

shoulders, young children boxing and many more intriguing sights as we jostled our way through the crowds before heading down winding, narrow streets lined with pots, clothes and fabric. In the artists' quarter, we found workmen squatting on the engraving jewellry, hammering iron, dyeing wool, carving wood and weaving chairs and baskets.

Back at the hotel we met up with Abel Damoussi, a tall, distinguished Moroccan, smartly dressed in a red jacket with sparkling, mischievous eyes, his long hair tied back. Abel spoke perfect English and served as a guide to visitors to his beloved country. He would be our companion and guide during our stay.

One day he drove us into the country to see an old kasbah he'd recently bought that had been in the same family since the 12th century. Rounding a bend in the bumpy road, he stopped abruptly, proudly pointing ahead. "That's the ruin I've bought!" In the middle of the sunbaked desert, we could just distinguish a small castle-like building standing alone on a mound. "I'm hoping to turn it into a hotel," Abel explained. "And when the hotel is full and I need to expand, I'll add tents."

Expand indeed. To us, the whole idea seemed as remote as the forlorn kasbah itself. However, given Abel's enthusiasm, we realised anything might be possible. We climbed through passages and low doorways to find rooms with magnificent hand-painted ceilings. As we wandered over the ruins, Abel explained where he envisioned constructing the guest rooms, pool, and tennis court.

Leaving his kasbah, we drove along a rugged dirt road, passing children minding herds of goats, a woman dressed in vibrant attire peacefully walking her cow toward the river, and old men dressed in djellabas resting on the roadside, preferring the lazier life.

Before reaching the market town nestled below the Atlas Mountains, we came upon an old lorry laden with rush mats. Abel shrieked and motioned vigorously to the astonished driver who, thinking it was the police about to reprimand him for an overloaded lorry, dutifully stopped.

"Hey, what are you doing with that load?" Abel called to him.

The poor frightened driver, still thinking Abel was the police, mumbled that he wanted to sell it.

"How much?" Abel asked, and proceeded to haggle with the driver over the price of the mats. "Okay," he finally said. "I'll meet you in the market in the next town and buy the lot."

The lorry driver looked confused but happy— had he done a day's work before even reaching the market?

Abel returned to the car, chuckling. "They'll be fine for my kasbah!" Speeding off in a whirl of dust, we finally reached the market town in the Eureka Valley, where we were to meet up with the lucky lorry driver.

The dusty market town was crowded with Berbers and Arabs who had travelled for miles on their donkeys from outlying mountain dwellings to buy their weekly provisions. Some of their visitors wore gandoras that reminded me of the flowing robes worn by Roman emperors. In the marketplace, women wore colourful draped kaftans, while the men wore sleeveless brown, white or perhaps striped, hooded djellabas. Even more elaborately dressed were the mountain Berbers who wore the burnoose.

We parked the car on a rickety bridge and wandered around, waiting for the lorry full of mats to arrive. Ted and I watched in amusement as hundreds of donkeys tied to posts (no need for taxis here!) patiently passed their time in a dried up riverbed, before being laden with goods and taken back to their dwellings. Finally, Abel's rush mats turned up, money changed hands and arrangements were made for the load to be delivered to the kasbah.

✈

We decided to explore the local souk. Passing under the arch of the city wall, the past splendour of the city's fascinating history came alive with its striking mosques, minarets, splendid palaces and horse-drawn carriages. We went into the heart of the souk, down cobbled alleyways where we were jostled amidst the milling masses and were captivated by the mysterious, exotic smells of incense, spices and heavy perfume.

Craftsmen and young boys squatted in narrow alleyways, producing iron, silver, leather, and copper wares, and old women wove textiles and richly coloured carpets and kilims, their patterns passed down through the generations. Young men created wooden objects of beauty by holding lathes between their toes, leaving their hands free to carve their ornaments, a technique that has survived for centuries.

We explored another alleyway that led to the old grain market, where we found cascading skeins of wool being dyed, treated and hung on bamboo sticks to dry, creating a canopy of vibrant colours above our heads.

A weaver explained that tribal weavers had prepared dyes from local vegetable and mineral sources since ancient times. He explained the source of the dyes: indigo for blue and green; madder root for red; pomegranate rinds and saffron for yellow; and henna and a variety of indigenous plants for red and brown earth tones.

We continued walking over the cobblestones until we came upon the famous Souk des Babouches with its tiers and tiers of yellow and gilt embroidered pointed slippers. Joining the crowd of locals and tourists, we watched snake charmers, colourful water sellers and acrobats.

Spiritualism and the practice of magic were alive and well in Morocco. We came across table after table of incense, perfumes, herbs and feathers. More striking to us were tables displaying displays of bladders, entrails, dried lizards, teeth and bones, all items used to communicate with the spiritual entity known as Barakah.

✈

Early the next day we met up at the old airport with many of the journalists and photographers who had covered Rick's adventures over the years. As the sun rose over the Atlas Mountains, the Moroccan cavalry arrived, carrying their guns and banners with great dignity. By 8.15am, satellite equipment was cordoned off in one corner of the airport, ready to give the world a view of the exciting event about to take place. Exciting for some, perhaps, but not necessarily for the family!

By 10.30 the crew was ready to go and Rick and Per spoke to the crowds before coming over to say goodbye to us. Sam lay on the perimeter fence with the other grandchildren, wiping tears from his eyes, while Holly was quietly keeping her emotions to herself.

At 11am the door to the balloon closed, the ladder was taken away, and all fell silent save the whirring sound of four helicopters circling low overhead. A fire engine, standing by in case of an emergency, started up its engine and then, silently, the balloon rose. Cheers from the crowd left the family praying that the crew would be alive and well when we next saw them. We were comforted by that perfect, silent ascent. Perhaps in less than 18 days' time, we would find them somewhere safely on the ground.

✈

At 4.15am the following morning, Penni called from the London Command Centre to say the balloon was coming down fast in the Algerian mountains. She told me not to worry and promised to phone again the minute she had more news. An hour later another call came. They'd landed safely, though in rebel territory on the plains of Algeria. My imagination started running wild. What were Algeria's prisons like? Was there a British ambassador there? My fears were finally quelled after the Virgin ground staff managed to secure Richard and Per's release. Once they were back on friendly soil, Ted and I had no doubt they would start planning their next attempt!

✈

At the end of February I was off to London to join Lindy and her family for the Countryside March, a gathering of thousands of folk who'd travelled to London to protest the Labour Party's plans to prohibit hunting and shooting; there was even a threat they'd ban fishing too. I wanted to show my support for the continuation of the hunting tradition, which was so very English and had lasted for hundreds of years, starting in the 16th century. Surely this march would make Tony Blair and his government aware of the strong opposition to their proposals.

The alarm peeled at 5.30am. It was a dark, still morning. Thankful for no rain, I hastily donned sturdy flat walking boots and drove to Chichester to board a bus to London with other marchers who also wanted their voices heard.

By 8.30 we'd arrived in London to join a street full of buses carrying determined but silent people from all the Southern counties such as Cornwall, Devon, Dorset and Somerset, followed throughout the day by busloads from the rest of England, Wales and Scotland. The March itself represented the themes "Liberty and

Livelihood" and organisers hoped it would be the largest peaceful demonstration in British history.

With banners unfurled, we set off from Blackfriars and down St. Dunstan's Hill. It was just as well the streets were closed to cars, as people were walking about 30 abreast. This was not so much a march as it was a silent stroll, with youngsters, prams and the odd wheelchair moving with us as we passed under London Bridge.

A helicopter hovered above, while on the street hawkers were making a pound or two selling caps and whistles. The marchers' myriad frustrations were reflected in the many homemade banners they carried. Some messages read:

Field sports – our heritage
Blair beware – Blair be fair
Respect our rural tradition
I love my country but fear my government
Liberty and country life before politics and spin
There are no toffs in our hunt

On we walked, with time to admire some of the buildings around Victoria Embankment. Big Ben struck 10am in the distance whilst whistles, horns and bagpipes blared and the march moved ahead.

From a side street we heard a Tertian band. This one was from Austria; they had come to march with various other nationalities including Swedes, New Zealanders, Maltese and Americans. The crush barriers were moved aside as more people and families joined the crowd.

During the entire march we noticed only one group of dissenters, about 30 anti-hunt protestors hanging over a wall with a placard, "Go home scum!" They didn't look a happy lot!

From time to time my mobile would ring; it was Lindy or one of the grandchildren telling me where they'd got to on the march and asking me how was I getting on. I assured them I was doing fine and keeping my own pace.

I looked up at a giant video screen that depicted wave upon wave of marchers as we approached Whitehall, where more banners glittered in the autumn sunlight with their messages for the powers-that-be:

Farming cares for the countryside
Abolish politicians, not hunting
Hunting is natural, even foxes do it
I march for freedom
Will they ban sex next?
Leave cowshit in the country and bullshit in Parliament

We also noticed a placard on the back of a little boy riding on his father's shoulders: "Mr. Blair please let there be a farm for me when I grow up!" And on another placard carried by a child: "Save the countryside please for me!"

As we passed the London Eye, we saw The HMS President moored on the Thames with a band on board playing stirring tunes. Meanwhile, the two marches representing the twin themes of "Liberty and Livelihood" were converging on Whitehall. It was a great river of humanity and each head was being counted by tellers as they crossed the line. In the centre of Whitehall stood a lone Scotsman in his kilt, playing his bagpipes, oblivious to the masses passing him by.

Now marchers were moving about 100 abreast. As we silently passed the Cenotaph, the sun shone down as we bowed our heads acknowledging "the Glorious Dead". Yes, I thought, today we were marching to preserve the freedom for which they died. Beyond the Cenotaph, the marchers separated, with "Livelihood" heading south over Westminster Bridge and "Liberty" moving toward Victoria. We learned later that the final headcount was 407,791!

By the time we'd reached the House of Commons, the crowd broke out into cheers, whistles and applause. Once we passed over Westminster Bridge, the hoard of marchers slowly dispersed, finding their way home. This march surely represented people from all walks of life, intent on protecting and conserving their communities, their culture and their children's future. As we walked from the Strand to Hyde Park, I felt cheerful, warmed by the bright winter sunshine. Would the government now realise the strength of country folk? We were not willing to let old traditions die.

✈

In June Ted and I were back in Morocco, hosted again by our friend Abel, to wait for Richard and Per as they prepared for their next attempt. Whilst waiting for the weather window, we enjoyed golf at the Royal Golf Club on a course lined with eucalyptus, orange and lemon trees. We also met a breeder for Arabian stallions and saw stable upon stable of those magnificent creatures.

The highlight of the trip for me was taking a drive into the Atlas Mountains, where Abel told us we must see the magnificent Kasbah Tamadot, which was for sale, as the owner was moving to America. We wound our way higher and higher until around the last bend, we arrived at a magnificent castle, floodlit and nestled below the snow-capped Atlas Mountains with a river winding gracefully below.

The Italian owner, Luciano Tempo, an artist, sculptor and art collector, had discovered this previously derelict kasbah and had enlisted a team of 30 local Berbers to restore it. He also hired a Moroccan staff and an English teacher to teach the local children, hoping that one day they too would be able to help him run the Kasbah Tamadot. The staff all loved Luciano so much that whenever he went away, they cried a week before his departure and upon his return, he found a carpet of rose petals strewn at the entrance of the Kasbah to welcome him back.

This kasbah was more magnificent than anything we'd ever seen. Luciano had furnished the interior with everything from fireplaces to ornate ceilings that he had collected from all over the world. He had also designed other furnishings that he hired local craftsmen to produce. At the centre of the kasbah was a petal-strewn pool, whilst the garden abounded with peach, nectarine, pear and apple trees and an abundance of colourful flowers.

The place was gorgeous. My first thought was that Richard might buy it and transform it into a hotel! Luciano said that if we acted quickly, Virgin could have right of first refusal, because there was another interested buyer.

So I quickly I made up an album of photos and caught the next plane to England to meet with Richard. I arranged to have an early breakfast with him the next day, realising it was my only hope of securing five minutes of his time. So whilst he was studying the newspapers, I was thrusting my photos under his nose. "Rick, it's wonderful, you must buy it!"

CHAPTER 15

Anxious to get off to work, he finally agreed to buy the kasbah, but on one condition—that in the future, when the hotel was up and running, I would look after the children in the nearby villages. I agreed to accept the challenge though I felt slightly nervous about what that might involve.

Nonetheless, in a jubilant mood I hurried to phone Abel and tell him the good news. My dream was to see the kasbah as a flourishing hotel! Only time would tell if my instincts about this magical place were correct.

CHAPTER 16

I N THE SUMMER OF 1996, I was named president of the Royal National Lifeboat Institution (RNLI), a volunteer organisation founded in 1824 that is committed to saving lives at sea. Eager to help raise money for this worthy group, I offered to host a champagne concert and picnic in our garden at Cakeham. What a wonderful response we had, with 240 guests, all gallantly dressed in dinner jackets and long gowns, who came to enjoy freely flowing champagne and music on a lovely summer night.

It was a warm, dry evening, perfect weather for a concert. As the Chichester civic band played on the front steps, guests wandered into the garden to find a romantic spot for their chairs and picnic hampers. During the concert, in the midst of a beautiful soprano solo, one of our peacocks decided to chime in! The audience stifled their laughter as he tried to compete with his human counterpart. When the concert concluded, the organizers ran a charitable raffle and auction followed by dancing and a fireworks display on the lake. After everyone left, Ted and I sat together by the lake talking about the success of the event and the beauty of the now silent summer night.

✈

Not long after our concert party, Ted and I took the train to Portsmouth to join the crowds visiting "The Festival of the Sea," a magnificent display of ships that included my MTB-71. How proud its owner David Watson looked, having managed to liberate her from the mud and reeds of Chichester Canal. Now here she was, standing proudly alongside HMS Victory! I will forever be devoted to the MTB-71, the boat that gave me memories that will never die.

David and his dedicated band of supporters had worked miracles with the historic boat. Having formed the non-profit MTB-71 Group and having secured support from his local Hampshire County Council, he had nurtured her back from obscurity into a well-deserved bit of limelight.

Thus I was thrilled when Norwegian Motor Torpedo Commander, Alex Nordhaus (30th Flotilla, Norway), noticed her and asked if she could be brought to Bergen, Norway in October. What a compliment— if boats could salute, she surely would have! He also invited David Watson and me to come along to attend the dedication of the Veterans Memorial for MLs and MTBs, which we happily accepted.

My MTB-71 had ended up in England because she was badly damaged during an air raid at Dover early in the war. This caused her Norwegian and British crew to disperse, some of whom joined the crew of MTB-345. Whilst that boat was refuelling in the Shetlands, a German Messerschmitt spotted her and the boat and crew were captured and taken to Ulven, a remote forest in Norway. There one British and four Norwegian sailors were shot on Hitler's orders before being tied to torpedo tubes and buried at sea. After the war, the German officer who carried out the orders was tried and shot, thanks to a Norwegian who had been hiding nearby and witnessed the terrible scene. One object of our visit to Norway was to commemorate the deaths of the brave MTB-345 crew.

✈

Could the Grand Old Lady, MTB-71, really be returning to Norway, her birthplace? I was thrilled that they wanted her at the Veterans Memorial dedication, but getting this 70-foot vessel there was quite a challenge. Commander Nordhaus said he'd send over the torpedo recovery ship, HNoMS Valkyrien, to winch her aboard whilst David and his volunteers—plus Eve, the WREN—would catch a plane and meet her again in Bergen. David was relieved, as he had been reluctant to let her ride the rough sea.

So it was that I accompanied David Watson to Heathrow with the engineer, the ship's carpenter and the general organiser for the restoration of the MTB-71. After a two-hour flight, we were greeted by rainy, cold, windy weather. Our accommodations were on board the Valkyrien and I had a cosy little cabin all to myself. I was sorry Ted was not there to enjoy it, too—he was busy and unable join me.

In Bergen we found the MTB-71 proudly propped up on the quayside with a flotilla of MTBs nearby keeping watch over her. We were honoured to take part in their programme of veterans' receptions, concerts, church parades and a trip around the fjords in another MTB, travelling smoothly at 32 knots. During the weekend we heard many anecdotes from the 500-odd MTB veterans in black berets proudly displaying their medals as they told story after story of bravery—after all, the MTBs' primary responsibility was to defend the Norwegian fjords.

When we arrived at the memorial ceremony, it was bitterly cold, with mist hanging low over the mountains. Hundreds of veterans stood silently by, their colourful war badges a reminder of the challenges they had overcome to preserve freedom both in their own country and in ours.

Standing among the sailors and the brave veterans and their families on that damp, grey morning, I felt proud to lay a wreath from the WRENs, both in England and Norway, to honour the men who lost their lives at Ulven. Other wreaths were laid by the Commander-in-Chief of the Royal Norwegian Navy, the British Naval Defence Attaché and various Admirals.

The veterans were then taken to the sleepy coastal village of Telavåg, which had been the setting for a wartime tragedy during the German occupation there. After a fatal exchange between the Germans and some locals who were hiding two Norwegian soldiers, all the men of the village were either executed or taken to a concentration camp, while the women and children were sent off to prison. All the fishing boats were sunk or destroyed and the village was burnt to the ground.

There were many such terrible war stories, but the veterans and the current Norwegian Navy officers and sailors spent the weekend focusing on the more poetic aspects of their service, heartily celebrating the 125th anniversary of the MTBs.

That afternoon, the little group associated with our MTB-71 took the tramway to the mountain above Bergen for a quick look at the glorious autumn trees. A few hours later David Watson knocked on my cabin door saying, "Eve, you have five minutes to get ready! We've been invited to join the veterans at the Naval Base for their annual dinner."

At dinner we learned that the Norwegians were anxious to keep the MTB-71 in Norway but there wasn't a chance we'd let her stay. They were very understanding and arranged for her to be returned to Portsmouth on Valkyrien, whilst we would fly home to meet her. Before boarding the plane to return to England, we watched the sailors from HNoMS Valkyrien delicately swinging ropes around her before carefully hoisting her onto their ship for the two-day journey. Yes, we thought, they loved her too.

THE GREAT ALPACA CAPER

Before long, I turned my attention from boats to business—the business of raising alpacas! It started on a cold blustery November day when I found myself in the back of an old farm truck squeezed between dogs, beaters and eight members of our Dorset shoot. We chatted away, attempting to forget how cold-to-the-bone we were.

Whilst listening to "the guns" discussing farm prices and the latest EU farming rules interspersed with the odd risqué joke, I turned to the man on my right, John. "And do you farm too?" I asked.

"Well, not exactly, no. I manage a herd of alpacas."

Curious, I admitted I was not quite sure what an alpaca was.

John explained, "Well, alpacas are a close relative of the camel and similar to a llama. They originally came from high in the Andes of central Peru and Bolivia."

"But why should you want to keep them?" I asked.

"They actually provide their owners with a fine investment," he answered. "They are also loveable, quiet, and charismatic."

"But why don't you see them much in England?" I asked.

"Well, they are relatively rare in this country. People don't realise how economical they are, producing enough fleece each year to knit eight or so light warm sweaters. The wool is even softer and more durable than cashmere."

I was intrigued. "Do they breed easily?"

"Oh, yes, after 11 months' gestation, the female produces one baby a year."

Our shooting lunch took place in the centre of the woods in a cottage comprised of only four walls, a roof and two blazing fires. Eager to learn more about his alpacas, I made a point of sitting next to John as we opened our picnic hampers. Tired and hungry after walking the fields and woods of Dorset, I allowed John time to enjoy his lunch before plying him once more with questions.

"John, tell me, if I bought an alpaca, how much land would it need?"

He laughed. "Well, first they are herd animals so you would need more than one, but you can have up to six per acre!"

He went on to describe how their padded feet were easy on the land and how handy they could be in running off foxes in the yard. By the time he said they could be trained to the halter and bred solely for their fleece (and not meat), I was really interested. But where could I put them? I pondered, realising I had only two acres of cultivated garden, when suddenly an idea struck. Vanessa had just bought a farm. With four children under the age of 10, surely she would like some alpacas!

"John, I want three alpacas!" Quick to answer, he asked what colours I would prefer—he said there were 28 different shades to choose from.

"Let's make one black, one fawn and one white," I said decisively.

I was elated about this new idea and could not wait to tell Ted. The bubble of excitement was soon pricked by reality when Ted asked how much they were going to cost. I must have sounded stupid, as I had not actually thought about cost. I made a quick phone call to John, who informed me that three alpacas would normally cost £10,000 each— good heavens!—but he would let me have the three for £27,318.75, which would include a recently born black male, called a macho.

Even with the friendly discount, that sounded somewhat steep, but I convinced myself that—with a baby a year and the fleece—they should soon make a fortune. I was jubilant again until Vanessa gave me another dose of reality.

"Mum!" she said, "I don't want alpacas! I have already got four young children and 100 acres to care for—and many more responsibilities besides."

I gulped. Too late, the order was in. I would now have to take responsibility myself. "Okay, if I look after them, can I have the use of one of your fields?" She agreed, and I was pleased with this compromise until I arrived home and Ted asked who was to shear them, tag them, catch them and goodness knows what else. Good points, all of them.

Gloom was setting in. My alpacas and I were going to have to cope alone. However, a drink in the pub that evening helped to solve some of my problems. I met Mati, the temporary barman, a tall, strong, handsome ex-polo player who was looking for a new career. My luck was in! Mati volunteered to help me and offered me the use of his old 10-stall polo horsebox.

✈

Not long after the three alpacas were delivered—one black, one fawn and one white—it was time to take the mother alpaca, Blondie, to be bred. Catching her proved to be a nightmare. Having cornered the animal, Mati lunged to put her in the horsebox when suddenly there was an unimaginable smell: relying on her instincts, she spat all over him in defence. Chaos reigned. When we finally had her safely inside the trailer and the ramp was secured, Mati and I drove slowly off toward Salisbury.

The noise from the old diesel engine and the grinding gear change left no chance for conversation, but in time we found our destination, Windmill Farm. Rattling over the cattle grid and up the immaculate drive to the house, we found Sir John, an ex-General who had developed a fascination for alpacas and now managed one of the finest breeding herds in the South of England. He seemed astonished to see us both sitting high in this vast old horsebox, as did the large herd of alpacas peering at us over the chestnut fencing.

Mati and I released the ramp and Blondie was only too relieved to exit the trailer. When Sir John introduced Blondie to her mate, we looked on in fascination. Hopeful that our small herd would now be expanding, we clattered on home to give our remaining alpacas a good feed. Before too long, Sir John phoned to say the vet had confirmed Blondie was in the family way and was now ready to be fetched.

Eleven months later Blondie was looking very pregnant indeed. One evening I was sure I heard noises coming from within her. Up early the following day, I dashed to her field and to my horror saw no baby but a brown fox lying nearby. Disaster, I thought—the fox must have eaten the baby! Creeping up closer, I suddenly saw it was no fox but a brown cria— oh, the joy! Blondie had had a throwback! My herd was expanding; surely there would be a fortune in that field before long.

The outcome of this tale remained to be seen. When would the incoming column ever be larger than the outgoing column in my accounts? No matter, really, that it never did and my alpaca caper came to an end. Not only did Mati and I love those alpacas, so did all of Vanessa's children, who played in the field with them, romping with the babies and taming them to halter. The brown one was so tame that she would come right up to my youngest grandchild, Ivo, nibbling his cap whilst he stroked and cuddled her before putting on her halter. So even though my business endeavour didn't work out, I did end up with some adorable but rather expensive pets for the family!

CHAPTER 17

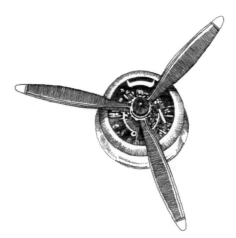

MY 75TH YEAR WAS A special one by any measure. All the family seemed to be on an even keel, so I felt I could devote more of my time to volunteer work. On one of my weekly trips to London, I met with Ernie Allen and Charlie Morrison, the founders of the International Centre for Missing and Exploited Children (ICMEC), an offshoot of their American centre based in Washington, D.C. I had accepted their invitation to serve on the ICMEC Board of Directors to do what I could to help generate awareness for the group's global work. Following the Hague Convention guidelines, ICMEC was attempting to help missing children who had either run away or been abducted and taken to countries where English or American custody laws did not apply. As a Board member, I organized several fundraising projects, including a benefit golf match in Scotland for a group of American donors. Richard also stepped up and provided support for their important cause.

In the spring of 1999, I travelled to Washington, D.C. to attend an ICMEC conference. There I took a tour of the American organisation's headquarters, with room upon room of video screens and photos of missing children. Telephones buzzed constantly as worried parents called for help; the Centre dealt with 25 to 30 new cases each day. One room that fascinated me was the Forensic

Imaging Unit, where a picture of a missing child could be reproduced to a probable likeness as he or she aged, year after year.

With treasured children and grandchildren of my own, I felt compassion for the many children throughout the world who were victimized by their own parents or other adults. Now that the Centre had international reach, I hoped thousands more children would have a greater chance to be united with their families and have the happiness they so deserved.

✈

My birthday that year coincided with the inaugural flight of Virgin Shanghai, so Ted and I joined Richard and Sam on the flight, along with 70 or so journalists. Landing in overcast drizzle, we were taken to the Grand Hyatt Hotel. Shanghai was becoming a highly industrialized modern city and small buildings were being replaced by skyscrapers. We stayed on the 84th floor of the 90-floor hotel and the views were spectacular!

Our hosts presented us with red Chinese jackets and took us to see the Yuyuan Garden, first established in 1559 and built over a nearly 20-year period by Pan Yunduan for his elderly father, Pan En, a notable figure in the Ming Dynasty. The colourful, lush garden is located in the heart of the city's old town, which covers 20,000 square metres and includes majestic buildings, pavilions, bridges, pools, and towers, with each of the manicured garden areas separated by "dragon walls". The garden was simply gorgeous, even on this rainy day.

Suddenly our sightseeing was interrupted by commotion and we looked up to see Richard pedalling down the street on a bicycle, pulling two beautiful air hostesses behind him in a rickshaw, followed by 50 or more cyclists wearing flowing red rain capes. It was a fantastic sight I will never, ever forget. That was certainly the frosting on my 75th birthday cake!

✈

Soon after returning home I met Lindy and Ned, now 21, for a smart lunch in London before catching a taxi to Buckingham Palace to a ceremony that would honour Ned. There he received a Gold Duke of Edinburgh's Award, which recognises personal development in young people. Both Lindy and I were thrilled and proud to be there with him on this great occasion!

✈

The next adventure was mine alone. Richard asked me to take his place in the 1999 Monte Carlo Pro Am golf tournament in early September. With a handicap of 29 I should have refused, but I'm so keen about golf that I couldn't say no! And a free golf game anywhere is always a joy. So my friend Moe and I attended and I enjoyed two of the best golfing days of my life, basking in non-stop sunshine, starting with a ride to the golf course in an open convertible.

At these Pro Am's, people are assigned golfing partners, and I thought mine—a rather handsome young man—was a delight. He was a good golfer and extremely gracious. It was only when the game was over that Moe said, "Eve, have you any idea who that was?" I hadn't a clue. My partner was actor Kevin Costner!

✈

Back at Cakeham, my friend Julia, who worked at a travel tour company, called to ask if I would like to go on one of their new adventure walks and write it up for their brochure. I was thrilled to be asked to join four professional travel writers who would also be on the trip.

"Me, walk?" I replied. "But where?"

Julia explained that the first trip would be to the Picos de Europa, a long rugged range of mountains in the North of Spain. These dramatic mountains rise steeply from the Atlantic coast, where the walk would end.

"Are we to walk over or around these mountains?" I enquired apprehensively. Julia was not sure; she did know they spread across 40 kilometres, divided by deep river canyons. I still played the odd round of golf and even tennis, but could I walk 40 kilometres? Walking had never been one of my pastimes. However, I thought, if my son can attempt to fly around the world in a balloon, it would seem somewhat feeble for me to turn down an invitation to simply walk.

Grandson Ned was the first person I consulted. After all, he had participated in a triathlon as well as the London marathon.

"Gran," he said. "You will need Gortex walking shoes and spare climbing skin. And by the way, don't give up for a blister or two. Remember they are only skin deep! Also take a First Aid kit, torch, compass, whistle and rucksack."

I was already overwhelmed when he added, "Oh, and also take a contractible walking stick, not an umbrella. And don't think you will get away with a nip of brandy! You will need to carry water not only to drink but also to use to wash your wounds. Water will also be a godsend if you get stuck in those mountains and have to sleep out."

Wounds? I thought. What wounds should I expect on this little walking jaunt?

Undaunted, I left on a Friday in late September for my three-day walking adventure. Was I crazy? I asked myself as I left my cosy home and boarded the three-hour flight from London to Bilbao.

Relentlessly hot sunshine greeted us when I arrived along with my four travel writer companions, who were all delightful but a good twenty years younger than I was; I wondered if I could keep up with them. We boarded a van for Alevia, a tiny, rustic alpine village high in the mountains. After a brief lunch, it was time to start our first walk. Courage, Mrs B! Don your boots, gather your rucksack and we're off!

Taking the walking guide and map, we wended our way up farm tracks and paths. Higher and higher we went, puffing and panting, with barely time to look back. I tried to keep up with the others, passing first a herd of cows and then a farmer on his old tractor followed by his trusty dog. Sheep grazed peacefully, their collar bells tinkling. Wild crocuses, mushrooms, blackberries and orchids covered the hedgerows.

With anticipation of seeing the sea from above, we pressed on, but suddenly the clouds descended. Oh, for a nip of brandy now! For a few moments I lost the others and groped to find Ned's whistle, but soon all was well as out of the clouds, one by one, my walking companions came back into view.

After another two days of walking, I felt tired but invigorated—I had made it to the end! We were all happy to celebrate before heading home and our host for the evening, Senora Benito, welcomed us back with a hot bath, drinks, and dinner that she and her daughters prepared for us. We enjoyed hearing local musicians perform during our meal: a young woman in a bright red dress sang and plucked the strings of a harp while her husband played various wind instruments including a gaita, a Spanish-style bagpipe.

After dinner, the sound of music outside lured us to join the local fiesta in the square. Under soft amber lighting we found children dancing and laughing, their parents and grandparents proudly looking on. Feeling happy but tired, we returned to our comfortable Asturian casona for a good night's rest. What a joy to have found this truly natural paradise.

✈

As the year drew to a close, Ted and I flew to Johannesburg, met up with four of our grandchildren and then flew 50 minutes to the Ulusaba Private Game Reserve, a property Richard had recently bought in the Sabi Sand reserve on the border of the Kruger National Park. Ulusaba (Shangaan for "place of little fear") would later become one of Virgin's more exotic resorts.

The children were wild with excitement when we arrived, running between boulders and through passages, discovering a swimming pool, plunge pools and wooden terraces that offered panoramic views. When we looked through the lodge's powerful telescope, we viewed five large lions drinking at a watering hole and a troop of baboons busily grooming each other while two impala, quite unaware of the others, sparred nearby.

We climbed into an open safari Land Rover and set off along with our Shangaan tracker Dyke sitting high on the bonnet, and ranger Owen Rennie at the wheel, his rifle always at hand.

Owen said wild dogs had been spotted in the area and he was determined to find them before they moved on. When we all looked rather disappointed, wanting immediately to find the "big five"—elephant, rhino, hippo, lion and leopard—Owen explained that wild dogs were nearly as endangered as the black rhino; the entire population was estimated at less than 5,000. The big five, he said, we could find any day.

Crossing the Sand River, we were fascinated by a large crocodile, more than 22 feet long, lying in wait to strike a leopard, a goat or even an unsuspecting native woman washing her clothes. The tracker suddenly pointed to the footprints that he said belonged to wild dogs. The hunt was on! Finally we spotted 14 wild dogs feasting on a dead impala. Coming to an abrupt halt, our binoculars and cameras ready, we found not only dogs but also a few baboons sharing their kill.

Some of these dapple-coated dogs with Mickey Mouse ears, who can pursue their prey at 25 miles per hour, were chasing each other in a tight circle. Around a red bush willow they played hide-and-seek with grinning mouths and bright eyes, oblivious to the people watching them.

On our way back to camp, as we approached a watering hole, Owen stopped abruptly and pointed to four eyes peering just above the surface of the water. These eyes belonged to two hippos who let out a sonorous bassoon note indicating their disapproval of our presence, so we beat a hasty retreat.

Ulusaba was a marvellous place to see this century out and the new one in! The New Year's celebration at the lodge was a joyous one, as the staff joined in with thoughts, resolutions, hugs and kisses, and we all toasted our loved ones, both present and far away. Making our own music, we beat the African drums and made enough noise to keep the entire animal population awake!

CHAPTER 18

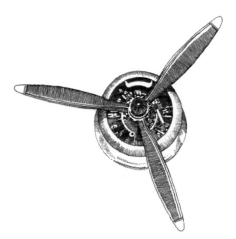

My article about walking in Spain was well-received and prompted a call from the travel editor of the *Mail on Sunday*, asking me to fly to Granada for a week to take tango lessons and write about the experience. Soon I would trade my hiking boots for black tights and a red rose!

A few weeks later, there I was at the Biblioteca de Andalucia in Granada along with writers from a few other publications. We laughed nervously during our first tango lesson. With three levels to choose from, I bravely chose the second level, thinking my dancing experience with the Rambert Ballet Company might give me a leg up, so to speak. Still, I was nervous as I stood at the back of the room while the teachers, Marta and Manuel, demonstrated the basic tango technique.

Hoping for inspiration, I watched intently as they smoothly glided over the marble floor. Seeing them reminded me of Sally Potter's film "The Tango Lesson," in which the dance was described as just as complex as its roots, and just as simple as two human beings moving as one.

The following day at the Biblioteca, we were instructed in the history of the tango and watched demonstrations by two famous Argentinian dancers who brought the lecture to life. I learned that the dance originated in Argentina and in days gone by, townspeople gathered each evening in a central courtyard and danced for their own entertainment.

After the lecture, our class met for dinner in the Plaza Nueva. I thought perhaps I should retire for the night at this stage, being of a slightly more advanced age than the others, but they persuaded me to join them at a nearby dance studio for a lighthearted salsa lesson.

The mirrored walls reflected our joy as we danced the night away, twirling and swirling to the pulsating beat, but oh! What a relief as the music finally broke into Tango, and we reverted to the graceful gliding of that dance, holding our partners gently as we moved as one.

The next few evenings we joined other tango enthusiasts at the theatre to see famous dancers, musicians and singers, all of whom had all flown in from Argentina to perform at Granada's Twelfth International Tango Festival. Our own grand finale was yet to come.

On the last night of our stay, at the stroke of midnight, it was our turn to dance. As the bandoneón player and pianist stuck up, we took to the floor and danced the night away, the men dressed in black and we women clad in black dresses, sheer black tights, high heels and yes, a red rose in our hair!

✈

Flying directly from Granada to Palma, Majorca, I joined the family at La Residencia to celebrate Ted's 82nd birthday. A celebration of another kind awaited us back in England when we learned that Richard was to be knighted! To think 50 years ago my baby boy was born—and now he was being honoured by the Queen. We were overjoyed as we celebrated Sir Richard Branson and the other honourees at the magnificent Roof Gardens restaurant overlooking London.

✈

That spring, Ted, who had been having problems walking, underwent hip replacement surgery, and I was impressed at how brave and cheerful he was throughout the process. After several weeks he was able to walk normally again, without his cane. To celebrate his recovery, we went to the Isle of Wight with our friend Anthony Churchill to spend the weekend at the Royal London Yacht Club. As we drove to the Folly Inn for lunch, memories came flooding back from the last year of the war when six other WRENs and I lived above the chemist shop in Yarmouth, sharing three watches. How different the Solent looked then, crammed with ships of all sizes, whilst now there was just a deserted pier crowded with tourists and barely a ship to be seen.

Anthony must have crept into the kitchen at the Inn to tell the owner that one of the Inn's guests from days gone by wanted to thank him for his generosity during the war. When the owner came out to meet us, we recognised one another immediately, even after so many years. I was happy to be able to thank him again for the boiled eggs he so kindly supplied to me and my friends, a much appreciated gesture during those ration days!

✈

In mid-May I got a call from Abel suggesting Ted and I fly to Morocco to visit the Kasbah Tamadot, which Virgin now owned. It had been two years since I had first suggested to Richard that he buy it, and I was thrilled that it was now a Virgin property.

Abel met us at the airport as we arrived once more in that wonderful country under a clear blue sky. That night we were invited to the Pavillon de la Ménara; it was the first time in 100 years that the Pavillon would be the site of a grand dinner. Candles were placed around the entire water basin and soft amber lighting illuminated the building. Red carpets led up to the palm-covered approaches and hand-woven tablecloths glittered with cut glass. Handsome turbaned Moroccan waiters served course after course as Moroccan drums held a mesmerizing beat.

The next day we went to see the Kasbah Agafay, the kasbah that Abel had discovered and restored. He had converted this ruined structure into a most unusual hotel, situated on the outskirts of the desert not far from Marrakech. Just as Abel had described his vision for this place when we first met him, the property now featured a swimming pool and tennis court and was indeed an oasis of tranquil pleasure.

Morocco is full of surprises, so it came as no great shock when we heard that Archduchess Francesca von Habsburg and her husband, the Archduke Karl von Habsburg, were staying in Abel's kasbah. Together with a team of volunteers and sponsors, they were working for the foundation that the Princess founded, Art Restoration for Cultural Heritage (ARCH), which supported restoration projects around the world.

Morocco's own King Mohammed VI was a patron of ARCH, which helped local communities care for some of Morocco's heritage sites. With parts of the Medina crumbling and old buildings and other architectural gems in a state of disrepair, members of the ARCH team were taking action to prevent further damage.

✈

One evening we were invited to join Abel's Kasbah guests, including the Habsburg royals, for a grand desert adventure. We climbed into Jeeps and started out on a rough journey across the desert to the site of the night's festivities, a deserted village that Abel had recently discovered where nomads once lived. Further and further we rattled into the night, with no moon to guide us. Other than a lone shepherd we encountered minding his goats, there was not a soul anywhere, no one to help with directions if we became lost in the vast void of the sands.

Finally, to our great relief, we saw a sign of life—a camel on the skyline—just before entering a deserted village. There we found Abel's team of helpers busily lighting lanterns, putting up tents and laying down rugs. Six handsome white-turbaned Berbers astride their fine Arabian horses stood nearby, reciting poetry and firing their guns intermittently as if to punctuate their lines.

A parade of local women sauntered past, showing off exquisite silken handmade robes designed by Abel's wife, Kenza Melehi. The braver guests enjoyed camel rides while others danced to the drum-driven music. Horses pranced between blazing fires surrounding the site. It was a veritable feast of culture and entertainment in this remote desert village.

As we relaxed on the rugs, two chefs appeared, carrying a whole sizzling barbecued lamb, which they placed on a platter before us.

Moroccans use no cutlery so, following their tradition, we dived in and ate with our hands. What a marvellous meal it was!

When we finally set off across the desert again, moonlight illuminated the way home for our camels and horses. This surely was a night of thanks to those helping to preserve the Moroccan heritage, the perfect tribute to a magnificent country and the talented people we had come to know and love.

CHAPTER 19

To CELEBRATE TED'S 83RD BIRTHDAY, we flew to Italy to revisit the sites where he had been a Cavalry Liaison officer during the war. In Naples we met up with Lorenzo, the driver who would take us to our first stop, Ravello. He drove us past the historic volcanic Mount Vesuvius, which we were glad to hear, had last erupted way back in 1944. He said only the occasional whiff of grey smoke proved the volcano was still alive.

We left the busy coast road along the Mediterranean to take the mountain route. Zigzagging our way through terraces of vines and citrus trees, we saw lemons as large as small melons! On we went, weaving our way through a grove of rich green indigenous chestnut trees. Lorenzo pointed down to the clear blue Tyrrhenian Sea on our last bend. With wild rosemary, cyclamen, orchids and honeysuckle on either side, we finally arrived at the town of Ravello, a lovely bit of paradise with a most magnificent view of one of the most inspiring places on earth. We walked down a cobbled alleyway and through an elegant 12th century portico to find our hotel, Palazzo Sasso, which featured terraces overlooking the bay some 1,000 feet below.

We had only a few days to explore the area, so we quickly unpacked and wandered down a path of cobblestone steps under lofty cypresses and umbrella pines, appreciating the refreshing mountain air. Lorenzo said that because the ride up to Ravello was so nerve-wracking, given all the hairpin turns, there were fewer tourists here than down below in the crowded coastal villages. In Ravello, there were no car horns blaring and no exhaust fumes; it was quiet, with clean air and natural beauty. Sitting on a bench in the evening sun, we watched children playing whilst old men sat in the shade nearby playing cards and young girls strolled arm in arm past the many ceramic shops in the town. As the shopkeepers closed down their shutters, we returned to our hotel for a delicious pasta dinner on our terrace, looking forward to the days ahead.

The next morning we talked over breakfast about Ted's walk down memory lane. He wanted to return to the beach at Salerno and retrace his footsteps from 60 years ago. The hotel had arranged for a driver to take us along the winding roads, through the terraced valley of lemon trees and vines planted in every spare crevasse. As we drove along, we saw, protruding from the stone cliffs, the remains of fortified castles and battlements that had protected the Italians from the pirates of the Barbary coast.

Finally we reached Cetara, a fishing village known for its grey volcanic sand. Passing countless fig trees, cypress trees and vines, we made our way to Vietri sul Mare, the town where the British Commandos first landed, hoping to lead the Germans off the scent of the main attack, which was to be at Salerno. Their goal was to cut off the enemy between Salerno and Naples.

Next we went to see the British cemetery at Battipaglia, where it was impossible not to cry, seeing row upon row of clean, white headstones amidst perfectly landscaped grass and flowers. Each headstone listed the deceased's regiment, name and age (most were under 30), and on each one was a short message from their loved ones. This was an emotional moment for Ted, as these were his comrades, and he vividly recalled landing at this beach with these men, with 88-millimetre German shells pounding all around them.

That night we enjoyed a candlelit dinner overlooking the Bay of Amalfi. Ted reminisced about his time in this glorious country so many years ago. We both wished we had more time to explore more of Italy's picturesque coastline, but we decided that the Palazzo had already stood for four generations so it should still be there when we returned in days to come.

✈

Two months later we were off to Toronto on Virgin Atlantic's inaugural flight to Canada. Richard dressed as a Canadian Mountie for our great welcome on the tarmac; it was an outfit that suited him perfectly. He always did love dressing up!

The highlight of the trip was going to Niagara Falls and riding the Maid of the Mist boat for a dunking under the falls. Wet and laughing in our blue macs, we were quite a sight. Richard let it be known to the press that he would go down Niagara Falls in a barrel if someone would volunteer to go with him. A beautiful young blonde tentatively volunteered, on the condition that she didn't get her hair wet. When she asked whether she'd end up above Richard or below, he could no longer continue pulling her leg. The poor girl seemed much relieved not to be barrel-bound down Niagara Falls with Sir Richard after all!

A TOAST TO THE AMERICA'S CUP

It was the summer of 2001 and we had taken the Red Funnel ferry to the Isle of Wight to watch the various races at the America's Cup Jubilee in Cowes. This was the 150th anniversary of the Cup and everyone agreed that this event would represent one of the world's most extraordinary gatherings of modern and historic yachts. There to compete were three J Class yachts; 36 sleek 12-Metre Class racing boats; ten International America's Cup Class; and many other yachts, both classic and modern, from all over the world.

How did this event happen? It all started on a cold winter's evening six years before. Ted and I were enjoying a midnight drink in Rawlings Bar in Cowes with a friend playing the piano and everyone singing around a blazing fire. Suddenly our friend Anthony Churchill started to go on about the America's Cup. "Surely we ought to be celebrating 150 years!" he said. The pianist stopped playing and we all took note of this excellent idea. Now, here we were, standing in a small attic room at the Royal London Yacht Club toasting the Cup!

Cowes was normally a sleepy little island village but this week would be an exception. The Solent was alive with hundreds of support boats of all sizes and shapes, It was exciting to see the start of the 50-mile challenge around the island, with helicopters overhead, the sun strong and the green waves chopping along. And the police boat flashed blue lights with its sirens hooting, trying to keep a clear passage for the J Class boats now racing, sails taut.

More languages were spoken that week than the narrow streets of Cowes had ever heard. The race to determine who would challenge the defender of the Cup began with a loud shot of the starting gun. Soon they were all tearing past the Needles, then Yarmouth, to a controversial and nail-biting finish between the GBR Challenge yacht, GBR 52, skippered by Ian Walker, and Prada's Luna Rossa, skippered by Francesco de Angelis. Walker and his British crew emerged victorious.

The very first race for the Cup took place around the Isle of Wight in 1851, with Queen Victoria herself looking on. The 24-inch trophy was known first as the 100 Guinea Cup and subsequently as the America's Cup, after the schooner America, which won the race and represented a humiliating defeat for the British yachts.

America's Cup has been a long saga of technologies, controversy and personality clashes over the years. The number of yachts allowed to enter was limited and each one had to be at least 40 feet in length, which is no big deal for the average millionaire, I suppose!

✈

Day after day we saw the largest number of historic yachts ever to gather in the United Kingdom. Being just a fan and no yachtswoman myself, I wandered amidst the crowds in the narrow streets of Cowes. There I found yachting teams made up of suntanned, muscle-bound young yachtsmen and women, along with hundreds of VIPs, media, and the rich and famous of the yachting world including the Aga Khan, Prince Philip, Gianni Agnelli and members of the Danish Royal family.

From the balcony of my hotel room, a telescope glued to one eye, I was able to watch the bevy of yachts competing in a re-enactment of the 1851 race. One of our friends described what it was like to be one of the crew on a 12-metre yacht: imagine the weight of a double-decker bus carried by the main sheet of rope wrapped around a carbon winch, which, as it was hoisted, sounded like a cannon. And this happened every time the trimmer cracked the sheets. Not too stressful!

The next day the main race took place on the 50-mile route around the Isle of Wight. Twenty helicopters flew low in the sunshine to witness this amazing sight. We watched the race from the water, standing on the bow of the famous HMS Bounty. Viewing this magnificent spectacle, I was reminded of a much different occasion, D-Day, when every available boat and craft of every size gathered in the Solent.

✈

Among all these sleek fibreglass beauties, one old wooden sailboat caught my eye—the Vanadis, built in 1868 and owned by Anthony Churchill, who had been determined to enter a yacht for the America's Cup. She was the oldest boat in the fleet, the world's oldest boat still sailing, and built on the lines of America, the yacht that won in 1851.

With a sewing machine on board to repair sails, a metal stove to warm the crew and oil lights, she was different from the designer yachts built to race in regattas off Monaco and St. Tropez. Oscar, her resident ghost from 1868, still tossed furniture around in a gale. Her crew had politely stepped aside, earlier in the year, to allow another yacht to finish first in the famous Rum Regatta, with first prize a skateboard and second, a much more desirable barrel full of rum. As old as she was, Vanadis, originally named Valdivia, was my favourite sea craft among the dazzling array of newer, fancier yachts.

After the day's excitement, we attended a magnificent ball in the famous Osborne House, Queen Victoria's summer retreat. All the guests, dressed in dinner jackets and evening gowns, arrived by water taxi. The evening was warm and balmy and the air was alive with music played by the band of Her Majesty's Royal Marines.

✈

It was just weeks later that we were brought back to earth with the horrifying news from America on September 11, 2001 that the

World Trade Center had been attacked. Only a few days before, after spending a wonderful week in Menorca with our dear American friends, Scottie and Holly, we had bid them goodbye and they flew home to New York. Seeing the collapse of the high-rise buildings on the news, we called them anxiously and were relieved to learn they were safe. But we didn't want to believe what had happened; the loss of so many innocent lives was heartbreaking. For those of us who had lived through the war, it seemed like a new breed of enemy had appeared. There was no telling then what far-reaching effects the incident would have, but it seemed clear that our lives would be affected in some way. Certainly, airport security would need to be tightened considerably, making flying a much different experience for us all.

THE NEXT GENERATION OF ADVENTURERS

By late October we were off to the Isle of Wight once more, this time to watch Milo and Ludo kitesurfing during Youth Week at the White Air extreme sports festival. What a contrast to the scene during the America's Cup, which was a glittering crush of yachting glitz and glamour. At this peaceful little seaside resort of Yaverland, we found the shore full of tents, cars and wiry, barefoot young men in seal-black wet suits, all busily preparing their kites on the green lawn. Younger fellows whizzed dangerously past on skateboards, pulled by miniature kites. Twisting, turning, and jumping the slightest obstacle, they hoped they too might one day become kitesurfing champions. The music blared forth from a nearby van, whilst other vans and tents were open for business, selling soup, hot dogs, and clothing.

The white cliffs of Yaverland were shining through the cold mist as the sun broke through. Out at sea, container ships, steamers and the odd cruise ship drifted by, all of them unaware of the exciting activities taking place on shore. Situated on the southeast corner of the Isle of Wight, Yaverland was chosen for the event because of its ideal weather conditions. The setting and weather were perfect indeed, and we were somewhat surprised there were so few spectators.

This was the first time I'd witnessed kitesurfing and I looked on with awe, seeing these youngsters leave the beach complete with corseted harness, hook, and wetsuit, and a board under one arm, their free hand holding the control bar for the launch of the kite that would draw them into the sea. With the slightest wind, the acceleration happened instantly, propelling them to 25 to 30 miles an hour, each jump lasting up to 10 seconds.

We watched them in motion, our adrenaline surging along with theirs as they flew over the waves, hair flowing in rhythm with their movements. They were carried up into the air, turning and twisting, even riding upside down before gliding back on the wave, with their feet still attached to their boards. Hither and thither the kite took them frontwards, sideways, backwards or sometimes on a three-swivel turn. At times they took their hand off of the control bar as the kite swept them back toward the beach. How the judges managed to follow and evaluate their movements was beyond me, and I'm sure they must have had trouble distinguishing between my 15-year-old, look-a-like twin grandsons!

The best kitesurfers fly for more than 25 metres, performing and enjoying endless manoeuvres such as back loops and 360-degree spins. The routine that made me gasp was "The Dead Man". Reaching full speed, the kitesurfer turns upside down, lets go the control bar, and then, hanging by his hook, catches the control bar again and rights himself! I must say it reminded me of my ill-fated attempt at flying a glider all those years ago.

It was comforting when the security patrol officer, nicknamed "Bombardier the Tractor," pulled his jet ski down to the water. There he'd ride wave after wave, eyes alert, ready to come to the rescue lest anyone was in trouble, for this can be a dangerous sport not only for the pilots themselves but also for other kitesurfers and beachgoers nearby.

The finals of the White Air competition took place on Friday. The sun was bright, with a strong easterly onshore wind, excellent weather for the top 12 of the kitesurfing elite who were battling against one another for this world-class extreme water sports award. Although Ludo and Milo were two of the youngest competitors, they finished among the top contestants, making their Granny and Granddad very proud!

✈

A month later, Ted and I returned to the Isle of Wight to honour the Poles for saving the island some 60 years before. During the war, the island was being badly bombed by the Germans whilst a Polish destroyer, ORP Błyskawica, was being refitted out at Cowes. The brave crew of the Blyskawica fired back with all the ammunition they had, bringing down a number of planes and driving the Germans from the island for good.

To celebrate the anniversary of that day, the Poles had brought over their Marine band to play in the commemoration service and in the Cowes parade. That evening, we all attended a Chopin concert featuring a brilliant young pianist, the granddaughter of the captain of ORP Blyskawica. Organized by Anthony Churchill, this concert was the first of its kind to be held in the new pavilions of the Royal Yacht Squadron in the presence of Her Majesty's Lord Lieutenant and his Excellency, the Ambassador of the Republic of Poland. The event was especially moving for me, as it brought back memories of my service with the WRENs on the island at Yarmouth.

✈

Could it be that the Branson family had developed a reputation for seeking adventure? Come Christmas 2004, a friend phoned to ask if we knew any boys between the ages of 16 and 20 who were keen on photography and science, as the famous Colonel John Blashford-Snell was organising the Kota Mama Expedition, a three-month scientific exploration trip up the Congo starting in July. Who better for the post, we thought, than our 19-year-old grandson Otto? I placed a phone call and two days later, Otto was down in Dorset for an interview. The happy result was his assignment as the photographic director on the trip. He recommended a friend who shared his interest in photography to fill the other spot, so the two of them would be travelling together.

The somewhat dangerous expedition, organised by the Scientific Exploration Society, would navigate Bolivia's formidable Río Grande, one of the last scientifically unexplored parts of South America. They would navigate riverbeds, which the ancient people of that region used as their waterways for trade, and they would survey and study archaeological sites in the region. Since 1998, the same core team had successfully navigated 7,500 kilometres downriver in Paraguay, Argentina, Bolivia and Brazil; this gave me confidence that Otto would be in capable hands.

No one had ever navigated the entire length of the river between Río Adapo and Río Grande, where the riverbeds are littered with gigantic boulders caused long ago by flooding, and one long stretch of the Río Grande is a raging torrent where the water thunders over boulders. Excavations near the river had previously uncovered hand-painted pottery and stone tools dating back to 500 BC and 1500 AD.

The organisers told Otto that he and his friend would be working in high temperatures in the canyon and would need to be prepared to carry their own gear and canoes. The studies en route would include archaeology, anthropology, biology, geology, palaeontology and wildlife conservation. Ted and I agreed this exciting expedition would be a once-in-a lifetime experience for Otto and his friend. Was he up to it? You bet he was! He not only rose to the challenge but he did an extraordinary job.

✈

In early April 2002, Ted and I received a welcome invitation from Vanessa to return to Morocco to join her family and friends for a 10-day camping and riding holiday in the desert. The morning after we arrived, Robert left to run in the desert marathon that supported the "Save the Rhino" charity. Vanessa and her children—Ivo, Louis, Florence and Noah, ages 6 to 14—were preparing to ride horses in the desert marathon.

We boarded two Range Rovers to see them off, making our way through the desert to the riding school where we found 12 horses and one baby donkey, tethered up and raring to go. All the excited anticipation disappeared and bottom lips began to quiver when the children were heaved into their saddles, one by one. An unexpected bit of chaos set in when we discovered that the stallions hadn't been gelded, and the mares, naturally, were over-excited, so the children, some of whom had never ridden before, struggled just to hang on!

At last they rode off into the desert, leaving Ted and me to pray and wonder at their bravery—or could it just be youthful naïveté? Later that night we were driven out to join them in their desert camp. They were tired and cold but elated as they huddled round the campfire, happily telling us about their day—all had gone well except one of the children had fallen off his horse. That was a hard way to learn that while the perils of adventure may be great, in the end, they're often worth the risk!

CHAPTER 20

THOUGH I'VE BEEN A WILLING participant in perilous pursuits all my life, being asked to go to the BBC to talk about my early experiences as an air hostess scared me most of all. At dinner with Richard and Joan the night before the interview, we talked about what I might be asked and I took down some useful notes. But I was so nervous that I didn't sleep all night.

Early the next morning a car came to pick me up and take me to the studio where the *Breakfast at 7* show was filmed. "Let me out!" I wanted to shout. But somehow I managed to stutter my way through the interview, after which I received a most welcome message from Richard on my answerphone: "Well done, Mum, you were super."

✈

I was delighted to receive an invitation to play in the 2002 Weetabix British Women's Open Pro-Am at the Turnberry Pro-Am tournament in Scotland and to write about the experience for the *Daily Mail on Sunday*. To be invited to play golf any time is a joy to me; to be invited to play in this event and write about it was beyond my wildest dreams, even if somewhat daunting.

After a short flight to Glasgow, a private car took me to the Turnberry Resort Hotel—it was a scenic one-hour drive through peaceful farmland. Along the way my driver pointed out places of interest such as Fenwick Moor, where Hitler's deputy Rudolf Hess landed after bailing out of his aircraft during the war. We also passed through Brig O'Doon, the setting for the final verse of the famous poem by Robbie Burns, "Tam O' Shanter." I was struck the breathtaking beauty of the Scottish countryside, a dramatic landscape full of history, heritage and culture.

✈

The next day I was awakened by the sound of gulls calling in the misty rain. By the time I arrived at the stunning Turnberry course, the mist had lifted and I met our pro, a pretty young Scottish woman named Mhairi McKay, with whom I and another two English women would play. In the midst of a flurry of buggies, clubs and caddies, we were driven to the 9th tee, which offered us magnificent views.

I was trembling with fright by now, trying to remember all I'd been taught by my young instructors at the Knightsbridge School of Golf. In spite of being the top British player in the USA (13th place in the PGA), Mhairi McKay put me at ease by telling me how she started playing golf at the age of eight and had gradually worked her way up.

In the past, the tailored fairway on this Ailsa Craig course had been narrower and Mhairi told me about one of her favourite earlier recollections there. Whilst playing with her mum and desperately trying to hit her ball out of the rough, a lone passing golfer remarked at her difficulty. She indignantly retorted that on the contrary, she found the course easy. The lone golfer turned out to be none other than Nick Faldo himself!

While still waiting for the start gun, I learned that McKay had won her first trophy at age nine with her sister, Fiona, at West Kilbride and how by 16, she'd already come down to scratch. Mhairi went on to become the first golfer, male or female, to win a scholarship to Stanford University; she said Tiger Woods followed her a year or two later.

Turnberry was Mhairi's home course, and she looked as relaxed as I felt fraught with fear! The gun resounded and we were off. Slowly I started to relax and enjoy the course, which hugged the rugged coastline, with its virgin sandy beaches, heather, violets and wild flowers, oyster-catchers, and sea seals.

Inland, one could see the remains of Turnberry Castle where it is believed Robert the Bruce, who became King of Scotland, was born. This inspired me to try even harder that day, ending up 13 below par. Not a bad score for three amateurs and one pro; the winners, all men, came in 18 below par. Could it be that I was a tiny help to our team? I like to think so! And of course I enjoyed recounting my golfing experience and seeing it in print so others could enjoy it too.

✈

In November, all the family gathered in Oxford for Holly's 21st birthday party, which promised to be a glittery affair with a New York theme. It gave everyone who attended the excuse to wear white ties and tails and all the sparkling jewels we ladies could lay our hands on.

Now in her second year towards becoming a doctor, Holly looked elegant and beautiful in a long white gown. She graciously welcomed all her guests and later made a lovely speech. After dinner, Richard showed a presentation of amusing snaps and stories of Holly's life, including a tomboy stage, though later she would end up very much a girl! All the grandchildren looked remarkably handsome that night and it was rewarding to see how well they got along. What a family to be proud of!

CHAPTER 21

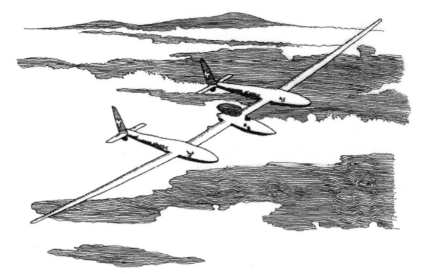

IN 2003 WE JOINED RICK for a helicopter ride to North Yorkshire for the launch of the Global Flyer, a replica of Sir George Cayley's famous glider, which had made its first flight in 1853. This replica flyer, with a 23-foot wingspan, had a frame of aluminium tubing instead of the original bamboo and a skin of hard-wearing synthetic material in place of Sir George's sailcloth.

We alighted at North Riding where crowds were gathering near a remote grassy slope. This was another of Rick's razzamatazz projects and we watched him, now alone at the helm, being pulled by an elastic rope for the downhill charge. On the second attempt, he left the ground, flying for 50 yards at an altitude of about six feet!

As the crowds cheered, children ran down the hill to greet Richard in the ungainly machine. This certainly was a one-off, but it was good old-fashioned fun and a great day out for everyone in attendance.

Our trip home in a helicopter with Rick ended strangely, however! We landed at Goodwood Airport in Chicester at 9:00 p.m., finding it completely deserted. Ted and I waved Rick and the helicopter off and trudged to the perimeter of the airfield. There

235

was not a soul in sight. Suddenly we realized that all the hangar doors were locked up and there was no way to get out!

We were thankful for our mobile phone. I called our son-in-law Robin and he and the twins came out to save us, shouting from over the wall. At last our dear grandson Milo leapt over the wall to help and managed to get us up and over the wall to freedom. A great day—with a happy ending.

✈

Soon it was off to the Bognor Birdman Competition, an outrageous event that had been raising money for local charities since 1978. Virgin had become a patron of the event, which was now attended by more than 40,000 spectators. Contestants competed to take the longest flight in a homemade plane—no engines permitted!

All the homespun aircraft were gaily adorned in the Virgin colours—mauve, white, and red. The Bognor pier and ramp were at the ready for the jumps that would launch the brave competitors into the air and sea. The weather was perfect; it was warm and sunny with a 10-knot wind speed.

I wandered down the pier, camera in hand, and crept up as near as I could to the end. There I could see 40 nervous competitors getting dressed while their teams were busily banging last-minute nails into their homemade machines—some funny, some bizarre, some ridiculous. The contraptions ranged from carefully crafted flying machines to hedgehogs made from foam and toilets or garage doors fashioned somehow into makeshift aircraft. Only England could put on such a spectacle!

Richard appeared on the beach, sporting a silver-quilted jumpsuit adorned with white feather wings. What was he up to now? One by one we watched the intrepid contestants leap off the pier. One woman had come all the way from Boston dressed as Wonder Girl and over she went, jumping when the green light flashed.

Up the ramp came a large helium-filled balloon held up by six Virgin staff, with birdman Richard in his silver jumpsuit. My camera ready, I waited anxiously until the green light flashed and the silver jumpsuit took off, but not toward the sea like the others. Oh, no, higher and higher it flew, with Richard's silver legs dangling below. Oh, my God! I thought. Now he's done it!

But no, there he was still on the ground, laughing. A few moments later, his white feather wings outstretched, he ran to the end of the pier and jumped!

The event raised £75,000—a day to remember forever.

✈

The next Virgin project would involve a much more sophisticated flying machine. Ted and I attended an event at the Science Museum in London when Richard and Steve Fossett announced that a new aircraft, the Virgin Atlantic Global Flyer, would be the first solo-piloted aircraft to fly nonstop around the world. Designed by aviation legend Burt Rutan and built in his facility in the Mojave Desert, the Global Flyer was the most fuel-efficient aircraft ever built.

Steve would be the pilot, though Richard would be standing by to take over if Steve fell ill before the flight. To date, Steve Fossett was the only man—then 56—to fly solo around the world in a balloon.

The craft, which looked to me like three seagulls stuck together, was made of modern plastic, as lightness was the aim. It had a wingspan of 114 feet and needed a 12,000 feet runway for take-off. The plane would fly up to 52,000 feet and travel between 19,000 and 25,000 miles in speeds in excess of 250 knots.

What a historic launch! It was not only exciting but environmentally important, as not stopping to refuel was surely the greatest aviation record left to set inside the earth's atmosphere. Wiley Post was the very first to fly solo around the world in July 1933 and he made seven stops over the course of eight days. The Global Flyer, scheduled to take off and return from a central U.S. location, would circle the globe in only 80 hours. And we hoped to be there to witness it.

The press release read: "At a time when British Airways was finally retiring the Concorde, the greatest achievement in aviation of the last century, it is fitting that Virgin Atlantic should unveil a plane which is designed to make the first great aviation achievement of the new century."

After the press event, I jokingly presented Steve with a huge bottle of vitamin pills, hoping that would keep him fit so that Rick wouldn't have to fly. He laughed and assured me that he was feeling fine!

Indeed, Steve did made the trip on his own, breaking the record for the first pilot to circle the world in an aircraft without refuelling. He embarked on the historic flight on 28 February 2005 from Salina, Kansas and returned on the 3rd of March, having completed the circumnavigation in 2 days, 19 hours, 1 minute and 46 seconds. He laughed as he climbed out of the aircraft and hugged his wife, Peggy, who had been waiting anxiously for his return.

"That was a big one," he said, proving that not only was he a humble adventurer, he was also a master of understatement!

CHAPTER 22

COME WINTER, LINDY AND THE boys and I were headed to France for two weeks to visit a few ski resorts there. We would spend the first week in Les Carroz followed by another week further south, but at a higher elevation, in Les Arcs.

The day before we planned to leave, Ted had arrived home from a 10-day safari in Africa. Richard and his friend Tim had invited their fathers to celebrate their 85th birthdays there, on an African adventure. Ted was still asleep when I hopped on my bicycle to get some euros at the bank in East Wittering. All was fine until, on the way back, I had a run-in with the curb. Disaster! My bicycle and I ended up strewn across the pavement. When I awoke I was in an ambulance having my many bumps and bruises tended to.

Should I cancel France? I didn't want to disappoint the family, so with bruises on my face, hands and legs—and a black eye—I left for Geneva with a suitcase full of bandages and painkillers. When we arrived in France, Lindy made sure I was well cared for whilst the boys went off to the slopes to ski.

By the following week I was on the mend, in time for our next journey by car to Les Arcs where we met up with Jack and his friends. By that time I was missing Ted, although he had phoned every day to see how I was getting on and I assured him I was fine.

As always, I was trying to improve my French. So when I met a young, one-eyed gypsy girl in a café in Les Arcs who was willing to tutor me, I readily agreed. We struggled to concentrate as I attempted to read French children's storybooks aloud while men at the bar sipped their drinks and smiled in amusement!

✈

Soon after the ski trip, Ted, Richard, and I joined Vanessa in Marrakech to see the beautiful hotel that she and her partner had created. She too had fallen in love with Morocco, and had bought an old building in the heart of the Medina. She was shocked when her Moroccan solicitor phoned her in London with the news that on looking through her deeds, he found that she had actually purchased not just one small riad but also the two next door! All three were included in the price that she had already paid.

After much thought and hard work, Vanessa assembled a team to create a luxury hotel, the Riad El Fenn, from the three properties. Eventually she also founded an annual international arts festival, the Marrakech Biennale, that brought local and world artists together in Morocco for art, literature and film programs.

Staying at the hotel was a joy: the smell of roses drifted up from the open courtyard and sparrows chirped happily above as we drank our morning tea on the terrace. Every day as the sun rose, we could hear the muezzin call the devout to prayer.

The morning after we arrived, we got a ride to the Palmeria Golf course for a quick nine holes. Ted drove the golf cart while Rick and I played. Because he was always holding the mobile up to his ear whilst trying to play, I beat him two-up. On the final fatal putt, his telephone rang and we overheard him say that he decided not to buy the *Daily Telegraph* after all!

✈

A week later, some of the family gathered to witness one of Richard's most unusual challenges—an attempt to cross the English Channel from Dover to France in an amphibious vehicle, a Gibbs Aquada. Two days before the crossing, he invited us to watch him take a test drive. He picked us up in Wittering at 6.30am. The dew was just lifting as we watched his noisy helicopter land in the field opposite our house.

Ted and I climbed aboard and into the sun we flew, with not a cloud in the sky. We pounded over the Solent and finally landed on Lymington Golf Course, where, parked on the course, we found a highly polished, black two-seater convertible. Could this be the car in which they hoped to cross the Channel?

Half an hour later we had our answer as we watched this strange car drive down the slipway into the river. Within seconds, wheels retracted, the sports car turned into a speedboat and Richard and his co-pilot raced off down the Solent.

The Gibbs Aquada gained momentum whilst speeding past the Isle of Wight and racing alongside the White Link ferry, at all of 30 knots, much to the astonishment of the unsuspecting ferry passengers gazing over the side. Surely that's not a car? They must have wondered what in the world it was!

✈

On the day of the crossing, the Aquada car team and several Virgin staff gathered at Dover for an early morning start. Virgin had obtained permission from the harbour master for this crossing, and there were numerous RIBs and Sunseekers full of cameramen and journalists revving up engines to witness the event. I imagined that Allen Gibbs, the designer of the vehicle, must have been proud of his six years of work as he looked down from his chopper overhead.

Indeed, by 7am, this high-speed sports amphibian, driven by Richard and Neil, drove down the slipway at Dover and into the water. When it reached 15 knots, it retracted the wheel coupling and used a water jet to propel the vehicle through the water, radically altering the traditional distinction between auto motor and marine transportation. It left the white cliffs of Dover in its wake with just the throbbing of 30 RIBs following, whilst overhead, Virgin Atlantic's 747 dipped its wing in an impressive salute. As it happened, this 747 was both waving hello and tipping its hat to the 20th anniversary of Virgin Atlantic Airlines.

Following behind in a high-speed Sunseeker, Ted and I watched Richard and Neil careen through the water and over the waves, approach the busy shipping lane and then cross into French waters.

I couldn't help wondering whether Richard knew on which side he should now be steering!

Finally, after an hour and 40 minutes, amidst great cheers, Richard drove the amphibian craft up the wooden ramp, over the sandy beach and onto the road. When he climbed out, he was dressed in a James Bond tuxedo, much to the delight of the spectators.

Until that day, the French had held the record for an amphibian crossing set in 1970, with a time of seven hours and 30 minutes. What excellent timing for Richard to beat this record. The day before, the English football team had been humiliated by the French! Now the French spectators were cheering and toasting as the town mayor and a representative from the Guinness Book of World Records announced the new record. The celebrations continued into the night, for it's not every day you can drive your car nonstop from Dover to Calais!

CHAPTER 23

ON 12 JULY 2004, THE day I turned 80, I awoke to the magic of Necker Island. The sun was gaining strength as I walked barefoot down the palm-covered passage and up the stairs to the quiet of the main house. I made two teas—one for myself and one for the only other person awake, Richard, who was already ensconced in his hammock, telephone pressed to his ear while working though a pile of correspondence.

I settled in my favourite chaise lounge, clutching my pen, journal and my French language books. There I sat in utter peace, listening to the sound of seagulls in the distance and the coo of mourning doves nearby.

After a lovely hour of work, my reverie was interrupted by the voices and laughter of the staff arriving by boat on the dock below. I took Ted his tea and donned my walking shoes and bathing costume for my morning amble past the hibiscus palms and wild cactus. I hoped to spot an iguana before diving into the sea pool.

Up at the house, the breakfast table gradually filled up with my family: Richard, Lindy, Vanessa, Ted, Clare, ten of my grandchildren (all except Otto, still in Peru) and my dear in-laws—Joan, Robert and Robin. Over salmon and eggs, they offered congratulations and gifts commemorating my big day.

Amidst faxes and messages arriving from afar, the skies decided the island needed a good drench and the rain poured down. I did not mind, as the warm wind was still blowing, whilst the family, unbeknownst to me, was rehearsing my evening surprise—an original production called "This, Eve, is Your Life," which was written and directed by Vanessa.

That night champagne flowed and white balloons fluttered from behind the long dinner table set for 26 guests. After dinner, family and friends watched the younger generation perform Vanessa's funny, well-rehearsed play. The last line, spoken by one of the children, was, "So Eve, there you have it, a life rich in excitement and love, a life of adventure and thrill. Who knows, it's almost worth publishing a book about it!" Good idea, that one!

✈

I've never worried about my age, but turning 80 certainly spurred me on to make the most of every moment. My first task was fulfilling my pledge to Richard when he agreed to purchase the Kasbah Tamadot in the foothills of the Atlas Mountains, which by now Virgin had transformed into a luxury hotel. I had not forgotten that I promised to take care of the children who lived nearby. So in September, when snow had just begun to fall in the mountains, I set out make a positive difference in the lives of children in the three Berber villages near the Kasbah—Asni, Asselda and Tansghart.

Villagers in that region were indigenous inhabitants of North Africa whose families had lived there for centuries and had maintained their distinct language and culture. Yet faced many difficult challenges, including limited educational and job opportunities. Indeed, what first struck me about the villages were the many teenage girls with no means of making a living on their own. At 13, if they couldn't afford the daily trip to another village to attend high school, they had no choice but to stay at home and take care of their younger siblings, or the family cow, whilst they waited to get married.

I was determined to change that situation if I could. So I enlisted the help of two Moroccan friends who were also my interpreters: Brahim, a local man who worked at the Kasbah, and Viviana, who worked at Vanessa's hotel in Marrakech. Speaking through them, I asked local government officials if I could bring in instructors who could teach the girls to make handicrafts such as rugs and embroidered items that could earn them some income when they were sold in the Kasbah's gift shop. My work would be supported by Virgin Unite, the non-profit arm of the Virgin group directed by the visionary leader Jean Oelwang. This group supports grassroots charity projects and implements Richard's philosophy—"Use business as a force for good"—in communities around the world.

The local government leaders liked my idea. So I returned to England for a week, taught myself to knit and arrived back in Morocco with a bag full of wool and knitting needles. The next morning, Brahim drove me and Viviana from the Kasbah up into the mountains in the hot, clear sunshine, passing terracotta houses as we climbed higher and higher until we reached the village of Tansghart. There we were greeted by an elderly Berber woman who invited us into her small home, a clean, empty space except for a few wooden benches in the corner. She invited us to meet two young girls, a few of her many grandchildren, and kindly offered us mint tea. We asked if she would like us to teach the girls to knit and she nodded anxiously, "Yes, yes!"

So we gave each of them needles and wool and sat on the mud floor. Within minutes, seven more girls appeared at the door and Viviana and I handed out knitting needles and wool all around. The girls learned quickly, giggling with delight; they were thrilled to hear that the needles and wool were theirs to keep, enabling them to make themselves scarves for the winter. On our next visit a few weeks later, we met in Granny's house again, and as the girls proudly showed off their scarves, the room filled up with mothers, their babies strapped to their backs, as well as brothers, sisters, aunts, uncles and various neighbours, all curious to see what was going on!

This time we handed out patterns and new "funky" wool, explaining that if they could copy my sample cloth pocketbook, we would sell their products in the Kasbah gift shop and a percentage of the profits would be returned to them. Another percentage, we told them, would go to their village association, which needed funds to deepen the well that provided water to the community.

Before our next visit several weeks later, Viviana and I visited the wool market in Marrakech and bought enough wool for our nine knitters to embark on still another project. But when we arrived at Granny's house carrying our big bags of wool, there was barely enough room for us to squeeze into the crowded room. Our nine girls had been joined by 31 more, all hoping to learn how to knit! Despite the parable of the loaves and fishes, there was no way we could extend the wool and needles to accommodate all the girls who had turned up. That was the day I knew my new life mission had begun.

In the months that followed, I founded the Eve Branson Foundation with the goal of providing these young people, and others like them, with the tools, training and workspace that would enable them to help support their families and in doing so, improve the local economy. In all the villages we would work in, we would teach the girls various skills, like embroidery and carpet-weaving, that would enable them to produce marketable goods. In each case, a portion of profits from sales would go to the girls and another portion would be invested back into the Foundation for future programs. I also planned to expand the Foundation's offerings to include English lessons, additional education and health care.

ROCK THE KASBAH

But where would we find funds to support our training programs? In 2004 I had met a very nice chap, Tim Souris, when I was in Morocco with Richard during the filming of a television show. Tim was a lawyer from Los Angeles who was working with the TV network filming the show. When I expressed interest in helping the girls in the villages, he said he would gladly help by holding a party in L.A. to raise funds. He suggested we call it Rock the Kasbah.

Tim put a committee of his friends together and held the first Rock the Kasbah event in 2007—a fun, colourful evening complete with Hollywood celebrities and terrific entertainment. To the delight of the guests and the press, Richard rode into the lobby of the Hollywood Roosevelt Hotel on a horse, dressed in colourful Moroccan garb!

Each year after that, we partnered with Virgin Unite and shared the proceeds with them as the events got bigger and more elaborate and raised more funds. As Rock the Kasbah gained prestige, so too did the guest list and it became one of the most popular of L.A.'s annual charity events. Salma Hayek, Charlize Theron, Sharon Stone, Kevin Connelly, Elvis Costello, Jewell and many others from the entertainment community attended to show their support.

Most important, of course, the evening enabled us to continue our work in Morocco. We used a portion of the donations to build a craft house for the girls in Tansghart. A small living area upstairs provided a comfortable living space for volunteer teachers from the UK and elsewhere who generously donated their time to teach the girls patchwork, knitting, spinning and other crafts.

The proceeds from Rock the Kasbah also enabled me to purchase 30 white Cashmere goats with the intention of bringing them to Morocco right away. I was wishfully thinking that this would be an easy way to provide our program with its own homegrown source of wool. But after a year of filling out documents to get permission to transport them from the UK, their number had doubled to 60! When the goats did arrive in Tansghart, it was worth the wait, as these lovely white creatures provided the girls with beautiful wool to spin and then use to create elegant bedroom slippers and scarves. Together with hand-embroidered crafts and carpets from the other villages, these items were favorites among the Kasbah guests.

But there was more to do when I visited Imskar, a village in the higher Atlas Mountains that had no electricity, no water, no roads and no medical facilities. What it did have was a population of young girls who were anxious to be taught crafts so they could become self-reliant. With funds from Rock the Kasbah, the Foundation was able to purchase a plot of land, the site of a second craft house that would provide a sustainable enterprise for the villagers.

A VISIT BY THE ELDERS

In 2009, I had the good fortune to be present at the Kasbah Tamadot during a meeting of the Elders, a group of visionary world leaders who use their wisdom and experience to work for the benefit of humanity. The group was founded by Nelson Mandela, his wife Graça Machel, musician Peter Gabriel and Richard. Their efforts and initiatives were organised and supported by Virgin Unite. Present at the Kasbah meeting were eight world-renowned dignitaries: Archbishop Desmond Tutu, activist and philanthropist Ela Bhatt, diplomat Lakhdar Brahimi, former Prime Minister of Norway Gro Brundtland, former President of Brazil Fernando Henrique Cardoso, former United States President Jimmy Carter, former President of Ireland Mary Robinson and Graça Machel.

When they took a break from their discussions, they expressed interest in visiting the craft house in Tansghart to see what the girls were making. Some of them went over in cars but others followed me on foot, walking down to the riverbed and then up the opposite slope. Climbing higher and higher, we stopped to visit my white Cashmere goats, one of which had produced a kid that morning! I said I would call her Graça after Nelson Mandela's wife, who cuddled the little blue-eyed bundle of white fluff. The little kid, who didn't seem too happy to be cuddled, let out a plaintive "Mama!"

As we moved further up the mountain to the workshop where 40 girls were busy making crafts, it was clear that special guests were arriving, as the remote village was swarming with security personnel and villagers strained to get a look from every window and rooftop. As the group neared the centre of the village, a group of children appeared, one child beating an old tin drum whilst another handed us a tray decorated with flowers and yet another offered a dish of local dates.

Inside the craft house, the Elders arrived one by one to see the girls at work. With the help of an interpreter, the girls' English teacher Zoubair, I explained how I'd started with a few girls sitting on Granny's mud floor up in the valley whilst I taught them to knit, a skill I had only just learned myself! The Elders graciously complimented the girls on their work and praised the concept of giving people the tools they need to help themselves. It was a proud moment for me and the girls, to have such esteemed visitors appreciate our efforts.

LOSING TED

On 20 March 2011, I was in Miami working with my editor on this memoir. After two days there, I was awakened at 3.00am by a phone call from Sue, our housekeeper at Cakeham, to say that Ted had died in his sleep the night before. It was a mercifully quiet and peaceful ending but still an unexpected and terrific shock. At age 93, my dear husband and confidant of 62 years was gone.

I hastily packed my things to catch the next plane home, though it was hard to imagine going back to Cakeham without finding Ted there, waiting to discuss whatever was on our minds. We had a private burial near Cakeham for the family—it was a sad and moving day. A few months later, it was comforting when the children organised a wonderful memorial service in London that was full of happy memories and laughter, which is just what Ted would have wanted.

In his memory, I placed a lovely wooden bench in the garden beneath our flat in London that overlooks the Thames. The bench, which I hope will be enjoyed by many, is engraved with his name, and was christened one evening when family and friends gathered there to make a champagne toast to this extraordinary man. I often go there on my morning walk to sit for a few minutes and remember special moments from our life together.

Ted followed all of Richard's exploits with immense interest and pride and I'm sorry he couldn't fly in the Virgin Galactic spaceship as a final grand adventure. That leaves me to go up on my own, in the mother ship, to send the astronauts—including Richard, Holly, and Sam—on their way! I have no doubt that Ted will be there in spirit, too, cheering them on.

NECKER IN FLAMES

In August I went to Necker for a relaxing few weeks with some of the family and several of Richard's friends, including the actresses Camilla Spence and Kate Winslet, who brought her two children, ten-year-old Mia and eight-year-old Joe. All went well on the first day of our holiday, though Camilla's wayward suitcase hadn't arrived, so a few of us ladies lent her clothes in the meantime.

After dinner, a few of the guests and I enjoyed feeding the parrots and the resident tortoise, ET, who was known for tickling our toes under the table at breakfast, hoping for a crumb or two. Then it was off for a good night's sleep in my bedroom in the main building, which was known as the Great House.

But nature had other plans! Somewhere around 5am, I suddenly awoke to hear two loud cracking and banging noises. My first thought was that the boys must still be partying and I turned over to go back to sleep. But this was no joke—the house had been struck by lightning and caught fire, whilst the winds from Hurricane Irene were driving the flames! I first heard Ned, Jack, Milo, Ludo and Sam shouting down the corridor, "Fire, fire! Out everyone—leave everything now!"

In the next instant Jack was at my door, with smoke and flames racing down the corridor behind him.

"Granny, leave everything! Get out quick!"

I grabbed my Mackintosh to cover up and then my handbag and workbasket, but Jack said, "Leave the basket, just get out!" So I made a dash toward the stairs. It was a terrifying moment but I was not afraid—I knew I needed to stay calm and getting hysterical wouldn't help.

But it was dark and without my contact lenses, I couldn't see a thing. The steps were slippery and the rain and wind were lashing down while the fire was fast approaching. I was groping my way to the stairs when I realized that Kate Winslet and her two children were right behind me. Kate swept me into her arms to help me down the steps. I recall saying, "Come on, Kate. I'm far too heavy for you. Let me go on my own." But she responded, "No, you're not too heavy" and moved swiftly down the steps with the children close behind.

It was pitch dark and pouring with rain as the flames came nearer—the wind had reached near hurricane pitch. As I looked back over my shoulder, seeing beam after beam collapsing into the raging fire, I felt it was the devil's henchman chasing us.

Once we were safely down, there was no time to talk; we were relieved to be on the ground but the flames were lapping at our heels. Desperate to get away from the burning structure, we struggled through the undergrowth, the palms lashing to and fro in the hurricane winds. The children were staying close, their bare feet hurting from the scratchy vines and pebbles underfoot as we ran. My mind was racing and I didn't even realize that I too was running through the rain with no shoes!

Finally we reached the Elders Temple in the centre of the island. We did a quick head count of the 24 of us—yes, we were all here, though wet and shivering. Realising everybody was safe, we all started speaking at once, telling our stories, unable to control the adrenaline pumping through our veins. Poor Richard, who was sleeping in a separate guest house with Joan, had been awakened by Sam and immediately leapt out of bed and ran naked up the hill toward the Great House, only to crash into an unforgiving cactus bush on the way!

We huddled together at the windows of the Temple to watch the fire devouring everything in its path as the skeleton of the Great House began to collapse. It was hard to believe we had all escaped alive, but it was even harder to imagine the alternative. The heavy smell of smoke hung in the air and I felt elated and depressed all at once.

Then I slowly became aware that everything was lost to that devil, the fire. My writings from the past few years were lost, which were very dear to me. My jewellery, my special birthday earrings from Ted—every single thing I had with me was gone.

Sadly, Richard lost more than any of us. His treasured handwritten notebooks and many of his prized photographs were destroyed. But his reaction was extraordinary. When interviewed by the press, he said, "All family and friends are well, which in the end is all that really matters." He also said the mood after the fire was "very much the Dunkirk spirit," which indeed it was. How proud I was of Richard and our family and friends—surely it was their humour that got the better of the smouldering devil.

The next day brought a few happy surprises. Sam Cox, one of Richard's assistants, found ET the tortoise, who had managed to escape the blaze, though with somewhat sooty feet. And then there was a sudden shriek from Camilla: "Look, everyone! They have found my suitcase up in the Temple!"

Both Camilla and Joan provided clothes for the rest of the ladies and it became a glorious fancy dress party. All the guests felt so relieved that they spent the day laughing and talking about rebuilding the Great House to be even more magnificent than before.

Some of us went down to the beach that afternoon, where the boathouses, boats, and diving equipment were unaffected by the fire that had swept through the main house. A few of the guests said they were worried about me, but I assured them I didn't need to see a doctor. Instead I took a scuba lesson, which I thoroughly enjoyed!

WEDDING BLISS

The rest of the year would be far more pleasant than that perilous visit to Necker. My children's book, *Sarky Puddleboat*, was launched at a lovely event at Knightsbridge School in London in early October, where my friend Magoo Giles is headmaster. I was delighted to have a book in print at last. Lindy, Vanessa and several of my grandchildren, including Sam and Ned, joined a happy crowd of friends and reporters to mark the occasion.

But the happiest day of all, and a perfect ending to an emotional year, was Holly's marriage to her wonderful boyfriend Freddie Andrews on Necker on the 20th of December, the same day Richard and Joan had married there 22 years before. Many of the guests slept on the beach, as the Great House was not yet rebuilt, but Richard had the house site cleared so the ceremony could take place there, on the same spot where he had married Joan.

It was a blissful and romantic occasion—Holly and Freddie were both stunning and there was love all around. I was moved by how joyous everyone felt that day, only four months after the fire. Having the whole family together was truly a miracle that I will always be thankful for. After the wedding, when I stepped away from the crowd to look out at the magnificent ocean, I heard what sounded like Ted's deep voice saying, "Yes, darling, life is wonderful!"

PARTING THOUGHTS

When my grandchildren ask me what I've learned in my 80-plus years on earth, I tell them that being happy is different for everyone. For me, the necessary ingredients for happiness are being open to change, having constructive hobbies, playing two or three sports, keeping an open mind toward others' ideas and thoughts, never seeing too much of one person, never being bored and always making time for volunteer work. It's important to have a caring family, too—nothing can replace the joy of being with people you love.

CHAPTER 23

I believe that one door has to close before another one opens. And it's no use wasting time on regret when there's always something constructive to do, including reaching out to others in need. One must never feel self-pity, as there is always someone out there who would gladly trade places with you. It's also important to see the humour in life and to laugh as often as you can.

Our lives are divided into four stages: childhood, teenage years, mid-life and old age. As one gets older, it is comforting to know that the rest of the world is getting older, too! I hope that others will be as content as I am when they reach the last stage of their lives.

But never fear—more adventures will follow. There's always another language to learn, another person to meet, another child to encourage, another memorable moment with family and friends, another galaxy to explore. And of course, there's always another book to write. In the meantime, Mum's the word!

ACKNOWLEDGEMENTS

This book would never have seen the light of day without the help of my close friend and editor Holly Peppe, whose patience, guidance and endless good humour got us through. She was the only person who had sufficient faith in me to see my work published and I'm forever grateful for her help and support. In addition to this book, she resurrected the tale of *Sarky Puddleboat*, one of my children's stories, from my piles of writing and published it in 2010.

For their invaluable assistance in preparing the manuscript for *Mum's the Word*, I'd like to thank Amy Newton, Penni Pike, Didi Colley, Rosie Buckley, Jemima Carthwaite, Jill Jephson, Susan Giffin, Evelyn Letch, Colleen Kropp, Alison Forbes and Laura Griffin. I'm grateful to Carrie Cook and Autumn Evans for the cover design, and thank Carrie for her chapter opener illustrations. I'd also like to send special thanks to editors Karen Watts and Kate Moore.

My appreciation also goes to several of my friends for reading the manuscript and encouraging me to move ahead with the project: John Whitney, the late Anthony Rubenstein, Tony DeMeric, Robert Deveraux, Miriam Moysi and Beverly Cousins. And finally, thanks to my son Richard for his valuable comments on a final draft.

Lightning Source UK Ltd.
Milton Keynes UK
UKOW03f0012150314

228190UK00001B/74/P